Joseph John Murphy

Natural selection and spiritual freedom

Joseph John Murphy

Natural selection and spiritual freedom

ISBN/EAN: 9783337277741

Printed in Europe, USA, Canada, Australia, Japan

Cover: Foto ©Lupo / pixelio.de

More available books at **www.hansebooks.com**

NATURAL SELECTION AND
SPIRITUAL FREEDOM

NATURAL SELECTION

AND

SPIRITUAL FREEDOM

BY

JOSEPH JOHN MURPHY

AUTHOR OF
'HABIT AND INTELLIGENCE'
AND
'THE SCIENTIFIC BASES OF FAITH'

London
MACMILLAN AND CO.
AND NEW YORK
1893

All rights reserved

CONTENTS.

INTRODUCTION.

	PAGE
	xv
Historical Progress	xvi
Europe four hundred years ago	xvii
Progress is not more rapid now than formerly	xviii
The profoundest changes are the least visible	xx
Encouragement for this Age	xxii
Drummond's *Natural Law in the Spiritual World*	xxiii
Change in Religious Thought	xxiv
Subjects of this Work	xxv
This Work not systematic	xxvi
Apology	xxvii

CHAPTER I.

NATURAL LAW IN THE SPIRITUAL WORLD. 1

The Parables of Nature	2
Growth—Parasitism	3
Degeneration	4
Environment	5

CHAPTER II.

REGENERATION.   6

Biogenesis	7
Imperfect Analogies	8
Spiritual Life and Death	9
The Natural Conscience waits for God	10
A Closer Analogy	12
Organising Intelligence	13
A Dangerous Admission	14
David Hume	15
The Faculties of Faith and of Science	16
The longing of the Soul for God	17
Life is not suggested by Matter, but Revelation is suggested by Human Nature	18
A consequence of Drummond's theory	20
Three Divine Kingdoms	21

CHAPTER III.

CONVERSION.   22

The Greatest in the Kingdom	23
Regeneration and Conversion	24
Peter's denial of Christ	25
Other consequences of Drummond's theory	26
Infant Salvation	27
The Children of Christians are holy	28
Spiritual injury from wrong theories	29
Instances from Biography	30
The Ideal of Christian Education	31
Vital and Spiritual Development	32
The Typical Christian	33

CHAPTER IV.

Two of Christ's Parables.   34

A twofold lesson	35
The Prodigal Son	36
The Elder Brother	37
The ideal Pharisee	38
Dangers of the Religious Life	39
Possibility of habitual Obedience	40
A Son with a Servant's feelings	41
Appreciative Thankfulness	42
Saint John on the Ephesian Church	43
The Labourers in the Vineyard	44
No excuse in this Parable for refusal of Service	45
Rewards are not equal	46
Temptations of High Position	47
The highest Rewards belong to the most unselfish Spirit	48
Faith—Works—Character	50
The Twofold Lesson of both Parables	51
The Typical Christian	52
The Fatherhood of God	53

CHAPTER V.

Natural Selection in the Spiritual World.   54

Error of Origen and Butler	55
The instructions of God are instructive	56
Butler on the Waste of Seeds	57
Not "a cruel platitude"	58
Darwin on the waste of seeds	59
Organic Evolution	60
Natural Selection	61

	PAGE
Divergence of Character	62
How far Darwinism is established	63
Difficulty of the Waste of Seeds cleared up	64
Improvement is from isolated beginnings	65
No Purpose of Equality	66
The same Principles in Human Life	67
To those who have, more is given	68
The Parable of the Pounds	69
Dissatisfaction with this principle	70
Progress comes of individual excellence	71
The Chosen People	72
Election, a Fact of Nature	73
The same principles probably act in the Eternal World	74
NOTE—Seebohm on Natural Selection	76

CHAPTER VI.

THE FINAL DESTINY OF THE REJECTED.   77

All Suffering tends to an End	78
Hope for the rejected	79
The Highest Morality is not Darwinian	80
The first steps towards Equality	81
Texts to be weighed, not counted	82
God has Eternity to work in	83
Narrowness of Vision in the Elect	84
The Restoration of the Heathen	86
Ezekiel, Jeremiah, Isaiah	87
The Sentence on the Serpent	88
Saint Peter on Final Restoration	89
Saint Paul on the same	90
Bodily and Spiritual Death	91
Abolition of Death	92

Contents.

	PAGE
Grace more abundant than Sin	93
All things reconciled to God	94
Christ the Saviour of All	95
The Future of Israel	96
Mercy coextensive with disobedience	97
Saint Paul and Saint James on the doctrine of Firstfruits	98
The salvation of all Israel and all Mankind	100
Meaning of Eternal	102
No Eternal Death	103
Chastisement, not Vengeance, in Christ's Parable of Judgment	104
Symbolic Meanings of Fire	106
Destruction and Purification	107
The Worm and the Fire	108
Salvation by Fire	109
Salvation in a Future Life	110
The Lost Sheep—The Lost Coin	111
Christ will give Eternal Life to all	112
Teaching of the Apocalypse	113
Apparent Contradiction	114
Death no barrier to God's mercy	115
The Gospel preached to the dead	116
The Unpardonable Sin	117
Forgiveness for Sins of Ignorance	118
The Larger Hope is best for the Elect	119
Ancient and Modern Difficulties	120
Note A.—The Firstfruits and the Firstborn	120
Note B.—Westcott on Unpardonable Sin	121
All things possible with God	122
"Sin unto Death"	123
Chastisement the way to Restoration	124

CHAPTER VII.

Retribution and Forgiveness. 125

	PAGE
The Prayer of Solomon	126
The Prophecies of Ezekiel	127
Retribution with Forgiveness	128
Jeremiah on Forgiveness	129
Saint Paul on Law and Gospel	130
Mercy through Punishment	131

CHAPTER VIII.

The Letter and the Spirit. 132

Saint Paul on the Letter and the Spirit	133
The same in a lower sphere	134
Christ on the Letter and the Spirit	135
Christ's use of Scripture	136
The Sadducees on the Resurrection	137
Similar Materialism among Christians	138
Christ's argument for the Resurrection	139
Christ condescending to give reasons	140
Worship of the Letter	141
"Not beyond the things written"	142
No worship of the Letter in Saint Paul	143
Christ's application of this principle in practice	144
Instances from the Gospels	146
Faith outrunning its commission	147
Faith and Love hope all things	148
Appeal from the Letter to the Spirit	149
Omnipotent Love	150
Christ's appeal to Conscience	151

Contents.

	PAGE
What may be expected in Revelation	152
First Judgment, then Mercy	153
This is what is revealed	154
NOTE—Saint Ignatius on the Letter and the Spirit	154

CHAPTER IX.

SAINT PAUL ON PREDESTINATION. 156

Epistle to the Philippians	157
Apparent contradiction	158
The question formulised	159
Meaning of Election in Saint Paul's writings	160
No formulated Doctrine	162
Jacob and Esau	163
Pharaoh	164
The Potter and the Clay	165
Saint Paul admits that the illustration is incomplete	166
Use of the word Reprobation	168
NOTE—"The Potter and the Clay"	168

CHAPTER X.

A PHYSICAL THEORY OF MORAL FREEDOM. 170

The question of Freedom still open	171
Statement of the question by Delbœuf	172
Difficulty seen by Descartes	173
Conservation of Energy	174
Instances from Mechanism	175
Sir John Herschel on the subject	176
Prof. Sabatier on the same	177
Brownian motions	178

Boussinesq's Mathematical Argument	179
Singular Solutions	180
Room for Voluntary Determination	181
Indetermination in Organic Variability	182
Organisms and Crystals	183
Delbœuf on the *modus operandi* of Freedom	184
Energy stored in the Organism	186
Mechanism of the Nervous System	187
Purely directive function of Will	188
Self-control	189
Evolution of Will	190
A Dog Pointing	191
Huxley on Necessity and Freedom	192
Fate is as hypothetical as Freedom	193
Automatism denies that Will can be an Agent	194
Paradoxical character of Automatism	196
Romanes on Automatism	197
Direct affirmation of Consciousness	198
Automatism removes no difficulty	199
How Automatism differs from the old Necessarianism	200
Free Will and Providential Action	202
Kennedy's Donnellan Lectures	203

CHAPTER XI.

The Reality of Knowledge. 204

The Problem of Knowledge	205
Metaphysical Error	206
Sensation, the ultimate Mystery	207
The two factors of Knowledge	208
Substance and Form in Thought	209
Kant's Agnosticism	210

Contents. xiii

	PAGE
A different point of view	211
John Stuart Mill on the Veracity of Memory	212
"Cogito, ergo sum"	214
Belief in an external World	215
Unsatisfactoriness of Berkeleyanism	216
Mill and Comte	217
Max Müller on the sense of the Infinite	218
Dr. Matheson on the same	220
Possibility of Revelation	221
Instinctive Belief of a Mental Nature in other Men	222
Data in one Plane of Thought and Conclusions in another	224
Forms of Thought were originally Facts of the Universe	226
Time, Space, and Causation	228
Locke, Kant, and Spencer	229
Evolution and Natural Realism	230
Escape from Metaphysics	231
Insufficiency of the Experience theory	232
Moral and Spiritual Intelligence	233
Faith is not based on Experience	234
Gnosticism and Agnosticism	235
Immortality the direct gift of God	236
Natural Realism and Spiritual Faith	237
NOTE—Kant on Space and Time	238
Kant's Idealism	239
The Divine Mind in relation to Space and Time	240

INTRODUCTION.

It is the merest commonplace, that the age in which we live is an age of unusually rapid historical change; and, in the most obvious sense, it is evidently true. But, like many other true sayings, it is generally so understood as to be in effect a fallacy. The changes that astonish us with their rapidity are conspicuous because they are superficial; but if we look deep enough, we shall see that those more important changes which are deeply seated and therefore comparatively inconspicuous, are not proceeding with more activity in the present age than in the previous centuries.

The changes which are so conspicuous at the present time are chiefly in the industrial arts; the improvements in those arts, which began with the invention of the steam-engine towards the end of the eighteenth century, have revolutionised industry, trade, and travel, and, in a great degree, the external ways of human life; to them is due the building of the vast cities of the modern world and the rapid spread of the European races over remote continents. If visibility were the true measure of importance, the century which is now drawing to its close would be, beyond all comparison, the richest in change and progress of all the centuries that have passed since history began to be written.

But if we look deeper; if we endeavour to estimate the changes which have occurred, not only in the surroundings of men, but in the men themselves;—the increase of knowledge, and the changes in those beliefs, sentiments, and ideals, which constitute character;—we shall arrive at a different result; we shall see that these profounder changes have been proceeding, with no manifest difference in rapidity, ever since the beginning of the modern history of Europe four hundred years ago.

I do not assert that this is a general fact, or anything approaching to a law of nature. Sir Henry Maine may probably be right in saying that with mankind on the whole, stagnation is the rule and progress the exception. The common idea about the changelessness of the East may be true, although the rise of Mohammedanism was one of the greatest and most rapid revolutions that history records; and it may also be true that the mind of man stood still during what were formerly called the dark ages—that is to say, the period from the close of the barbarian invasions which destroyed the Roman Empire, to the rise of medieval civilisation. But what are properly called the middle ages were a period of change and progress; and during the entire period of four hundred years that has passed since the beginning, towards the close of the fifteenth century, of what is properly modern history, that invisible progress of the intellect which underlies visible progress, has proceeded, so far as the rapidity of such a process admits of being estimated, as rapidly as it is proceeding now.

To make this evident, let us consider what was the state of the European world immediately before the discovery of America in the year 1492—an event which may be fairly regarded as the commencement of modern history. At that time, the greater part of the globe had never been visited by Europeans; and the existence of North and South America, of Oceania, and of the ocean route to India, was unknown. Astronomy was as the ancients had left it, and the earth was regarded as the centre of the universe. The fundamental conceptions of our modern physical science had not been formed; the foundation of physiology had not been laid, and it appears probable that medical and surgical practice had retrograded since the time of the Roman Empire. The Renaissance was only dawning, and the intellectual glories of Elizabethan England were in the future; the Papal and the Feudal systems remained unbroken; the religious revolt of the Reformation, and the political revolt of the French Revolution, were not imagined. The Divine right of kings remained unquestioned; and the enforcement of religious orthodoxy and ecclesiastical conformity was regarded as a sacred duty of the State. The Christian virtues of humanity and mercy were scarcely known in the political sphere;—with the partial exception of England, every European state practised torture in the administration of justice, and excessive cruelty in the judicial infliction of death.

Such, in extremest outline, was the intellectual and political state of Europe four hundred years ago. How vast is the change! Yet four hundred years is but a short period in the history of the world, and a short period even in comparison with the life of man. Many of us can ourselves look back over fifty years of history; and to none of us is it a period that baffles the imagination. Yet fifty years is one-eighth of the time that has passed since modern history began. But if we consider the changes, excluding those which are merely physical and industrial, which have occurred during the past fifty years, and compare their magnitude with the total magnitude of those which began with the discovery of America, we shall probably conclude that scarcely one-eighth of the total change of the past four hundred years has occurred during the last half-century; and that change and progress have in no degree increased their rapidity during the last fifty years of the four hundred. Or, instead of the past fifty, let us speak of the past hundred years. One hundred years ago the vast industrial changes of the modern age had not begun; chemical science had only come into existence; the possible powers of steam were dreamed of by only a few, and those of electricity not dreamed of at all. Yet the French Revolution was in progress, and men's thoughts, beliefs, and ideals were modern. The transformation of the medieval world of 1492 into the modern world of 1892, had been in 1792 accomplished to at least three-fourths of its extent.

But if the profoundest historical change is not more rapid now than it was in former ages, this truth is, or ought to be, obvious; and why is it not generally seen to be true?

Three reasons are to be given. One of them has been already mentioned, namely, the extraordinary visibility of the more remarkable changes which the present century has seen.

Another reason for the prevalent belief that progress is more rapid now than formerly, is that the vastly increased facility of human intercourse, by printing, by post, and by travel, enables information to spread with a degree of rapidity which was formerly unknown. I maintain that change and progress are not new;—what is new is the consciousness by society of its own changes. Men formerly, as it were, stood on a plain and hid each other; now they are visible to each other, as in an amphitheatre.

There is, however, yet another reason, of a different kind, consisting not in any external fact but in natural habits of thought. Although we know that fifty is an eighth of four hundred, yet we do not naturally and habitually think of fifty years and four hundred years as comparable magnitudes. We do not think of vast historic periods in the same terms as of the periods over which our own memory extends; we have naturally a vague kind of notion that the historical ages were not only much longer, but almost infinitely longer, than our own remembered lifetime; and it needs some mental effort to make it appear real, that the period which passed between the accession of our present Queen and her Jubilee, was an eighth of that which has passed since modern history began with the discovery of America.

But not only is the visibility of historical change no proof of its profundity; it may be maintained that the opposite is true, and that the profoundest changes are, to contemporaries, the least visible. God revealed Himself to Elijah neither in the storm, nor in the earthquake, nor in the fire, but in the still small voice;[1] and when Christ was asked when the Kingdom of God was to appear, He replied, "The Kingdom of God cometh not with observation; the Kingdom of God is in the midst of you"[2] (already). It is most probably a general law of Providential guidance and of historical progress, that the profoundest and most fruitful changes are wrought in silence, like the growth of the seed. The first conquests of Christianity were made in silence under the protection of the internal peace of the

---

[1] 1 Kings xix. 11 *et seq.*
[2] Luke xvii. 20, 21, margin of Revised Version.

Roman Empire; and though the period from the subsidence of the Reformation movement to the outbreak of the French Revolution was by no means one of peace, yet the wars of that time were not actuated by religious zeal, but by the ordinary motives of rivalry and ambition; and to that period belongs the greatest of all the changes that have transformed medieval into modern Europe; namely, the separation of political from religious interests;—a change which came without any revolutionary movement, and almost unconsciously.

To what purpose are these remarks, in the introduction to a volume of theological and philosophical essays?

They are to this purpose:—We are constantly told that we are living in a time of religious unrest and change. This is obviously true; and the consciousness of the unrest, both among those who welcome it and those who dread it, must tend to increase the unrest; but extravagant hopes and extravagant fears will alike be discouraged, if we see that social and religious change and unrest are not new;—what is new is only the widely-spread consciousness of them. It is well to know that the trials which befall us are only such as are common to man, and such as man is able to bear.[1] A Church and a Faith which have fought for life, and have prevailed, against both Imperial and Papal Rome,

[1] See 1 Cor. x. 13, Authorised and Revised Versions.

ought not to be dismayed by any prospect of disestablishment and disendowment; and the shock given to religious convictions in our time by the doctrine of Evolution, cannot be greater than that caused by the astronomical discoveries which proved the earth not to be the centre of the universe. Virgil's words may be truly spoken to us,

> O passi graviora! dabit Deus his quoque finem.

In the year 1873 I published through Macmillan and Co. a book entitled *The Scientific Bases of Faith*, with the purpose of showing that the new ideas of the nature and origin of things, including the entire doctrine of Evolution, constitute a better basis for Theistic and Christian faith than the old[1]: and some chapters were added on the special and characteristic doctrines of Christianity. The edition is now exhausted, and the publishers do not encourage me to venture a second. But during the twenty years which have passed since that book was published, much has been thought, said, and written, on the subjects whereof it treats; and the purpose of the

---

[1] The *Spectator*, in reviewing *The Scientific Bases of Faith*, said that the title is somewhat inappropriate, because the work is only a scientific examination of the bases of faith, and I really base faith not on science but on instinct. This last remark is quite true;—see the concluding chapter of the present work, especially pp. 222-225, and 233-235. But the title of my former work is meant to express the truth, that although Faith transcends Nature and Science, yet it has its bases in that Nature which can be scientifically understood.

present work is to set before the world my newer thoughts on the same class of subjects.

The best-known contribution to religious philosophy that has appeared since the publication of my former work, is Professor Drummond's *Natural Law in the Spiritual World:* and a considerable part of the present work is occupied with an examination of its theories.[1] I need not here anticipate what is treated of in the following chapters, but I have to remark with wonder on the vast change which must have come, unnoticed, over the religious mind of England and the entire English-speaking people, before Professor Drummond's work could have been received as an orthodox book. I do not refer to his acceptance of those doctrines of Evolution which are currently associated with the name of Darwin; the religious mind was certain to be reconciled to them, as it had already been to the discoveries of astronomy and of geology; and that it should be so is purely reason for thankfulness. I speak of a far different change.

There is not one of Drummond's characteristic passages which might not have been written by a denier of the characteristic doctrines of Apostolic and Nicene Christianity;—which, as I understand them, are the doctrines of the Trinity, the Incarnation, and the Atonement;—the doctrine that there is an Eternal, uncreated, Son of God, who is God, united with the Father and the Holy Spirit;—who took

---

[1] It is, however, by merely accidental coincidence that his book and the present one contain each eleven chapters.

upon Himself a human nature, and in that nature strove against the powers of evil, suffering to death in the strife; but was raised from the dead and exalted into Heaven by the might of the Father, to declare His victory, and, with it, the salvation of mankind. I am aware that Professor Drummond believes these doctrines, for he has told us so, and his honesty is beyond question. But he has told us so only in passages which have no logical connection with the rest of his work, and he has not made it evident how it is possible for an Evangelical Christian to write of conversion and salvation, without expressly basing them on the Atonement of Christ. The change which must have come over religious thought before such a book could have been favourably received by religious men, appears to be a new manifestation of the modern tendency to an exaggerated and excessive subjectivity—or, to use a more intelligible word, self-occupation—which in our days causes religious thought to dwell, much more than in earlier times, on the soul of man; so that such a work as Professor Drummond's may reasonably be complained of as containing little theology though much anthropology; much about man and little about God. It is said that, in the theology which sprang out of Luther's teaching, the thought of faith, and of justification by faith, often obscured the thought of Christ who is the Object of faith, and of God who justifies;[1] and it would seem that in the present

---

[1] Θεὸς ὁ δικαιῶν. Romans viii. 33.

generation there is a similar but even stronger tendency, for the thought of conversion to attract such exclusive attention as to obscure that of the Father who sends the Holy Spirit to convert the soul, and of the Lord Jesus Christ in whose name the Holy Spirit is sent.[1]

The earlier chapters of the present work are occupied with an examination of Drummond's doctrine of conversion. After these, I have endeavoured to show, what Drummond has not seen, that the Darwinian law of progress by natural selection among spontaneous variations, is a case of "natural law" which is also true of the "spiritual world." This raises the question of the fate of those who are rejected in God's selective judgment; and I have given my reasons for believing that the teaching of Nature does not oppose the hope of the ultimate salvation of all; while that of Revelation, when rightly understood, favours it.

The subject of Judgment and Responsibility leads on to that of Freedom; and I have devoted two chapters to the inquiries, what the books of Revelation and of Nature, respectively, have to tell us on this question; with the result, that they both leave it open and undecided, to be answered by us according to the light of reason and conscience. It may appear to some readers that, in these two chapters, I have changed my position in an inconsistent way

---

[1] John xiv. 26.

between the religious and the scientific points of view. But I believe, and have written my former work in great part for the purpose of showing, that the worlds of matter and of spirit — the truths of science and of faith — are much closer to each other, and interpenetrate much more, than is generally seen by the men of this generation.

The final chapter contains an argument which I believe is original, or at least stated in an original way, against both Gnosticism and Agnosticism, and in favour of what may be called religious common sense.

It will be seen that the present work is little more than a collection of occasional essays, and makes no pretence to systematic completeness. It will be seen also that I write as a believer to believers; I have not endeavoured to prove the truth of the Christian Revelation, or the general trustworthiness of the Christian Scriptures, but have throughout taken them as established.

I have to conclude this Introduction with an apology. In my *Scientific Bases of Faith*, page 197, the following occurs :—" I need not spend any time in refuting the wretched fiction of an imputed righteousness, by which God is by some supposed to account men as righteous who are not so." I now regret the expression "wretched fiction." It was neither just in itself nor becoming in me, thus to speak of a belief which is held by many who, I doubt not, are better men and better Christians than myself. I still, however, adhere to the belief that, as expressed higher up on the same page, "with Saint Paul, *to justify* means *to make righteous*"; not merely to account righteous. Compare Saint Peter's expression, "purifying their hearts by faith."[1]

---

[1] τῇ πίστει καθαρίσας τὰς καρδίας αὐτῶν. Acts xv. 9. The Revisers have unfortunately substituted *cleansing* for *purifying*, thus obscuring what is probably an allusion to our Lord's words, "Blessed are the pure in heart" (μακάριοι οἱ καθαροὶ τῇ καρδίᾳ) Matt. v. 8.

BELFAST, 22nd *March* 1893.

CHAPTER I.

NATURAL LAW IN THE SPIRITUAL WORLD.

[This chapter and the two following are little more than a reproduction of the review of Drummond's *Natural Law in the Spiritual World* by the present writer in the *British Quarterly Review* for July 1884.]

THE great and widely-felt interest excited by Professor Drummond's work on *Natural Law in the Spiritual World* is to be noted with much satisfaction; for it is necessary to the spiritual life of the community, though not always to that of the individual, that some degree of intellectual interest in religion be maintained: the union of intellectual with spiritual life is needful for the vigour as well as the purity of both. We are bidden to love the Lord with all the mind as well as with all the heart.

Yet the merits of this work — its originality, suggestiveness, clearness of thought, and eloquence of expression — do not prevent me from thinking that, if tried by the standard of its own very high claims, it must be regarded as a failure. Its claim is to set forth a system of religious philosophy; and though it contains much true religious philosophy, yet it does not contain a system at all, but only a number of detached though elaborately worked out suggestions. Its eleven chapters are eleven sermons from texts found in nature, all of them impressive, and all of them true except where exaggerated into something approaching to falsity. But a series of philosophical treatises do not necessarily form a philosophical system.

In the character of the analogies that he has wrought out, Professor Drummond's work reminds us of those parables of Our Lord which are taken from vegetation and agriculture. Perhaps the entire idea of the work has been suggested by them; and we must agree with its author that such parables as those of the Sower,[1] the Seed growing in secret,[2] the Vine and its branches,[3] and the Seed dying in order to bear fruit,[4] point to a real analogy between the organic life of the plant and the spiritual life in the heart of man. If an eloquent commentary were written on these parables, with constant and emphatic assertions that the truth of the parable depends, not on mere similarity but on identity of law between the natural world of types and the spiritual world of antitypes, such a work, in its general ideas, would much resemble Professor Drummond's. Some of his parables, however, though quite true, throw no real light on the laws of what

[1] Matt. xiii. 3.   [2] Mark iv. 26.
[3] John xv. 1.   [4] John xii. 24; see also 1 Cor. xv.

is properly the spiritual world. His chapter on Growth, for instance, is a beautifully-written treatise on the stillness and silence of all growth, spiritual as well as organic. But we have always known that these are characters of all growth; and in showing that they are characters of spiritual as well as of bodily and mental growth, he only shows that spiritual growth and development are effected under the laws of life and mind, and goes no way whatever towards proving what is the very foundation of his system, and indeed of all religious philosophy, namely, the distinctness of the spiritual life, and its introduction into the world of human life and into the heart of man by the same Creating Spirit who in the beginning moved on the face of the dark and formless waters. The same remark applies to the chapter on Parasitism, which is an ingenious, eloquent, and picturesque illustration of the truth that as animals, and even plants, degenerate when they obtain their subsistence too easily,[1] so it is with the spiritual life. Any religious system causes degeneracy which tends to relieve the individual of responsibility, and to relax exertion: such is that of the Church of Rome, and Protestant Churches are not altogether free from the same tendency. This

---

[1] The most remarkable instances of this are probably those of the Cirrhipedes or Barnacles, which begin life as freely-swimming Crustaceans, but lose their organs of motion and of sight, and degenerate into fixed shell-fish; and the Rhizencephala, which begin life in the same form, but become external parasites on fishes, and degenerate into the likeness of worms.

is true in virtue of laws of life and mind which would be equally valid if there were no spiritual world at all — if "the spirit did but mean the breath."

The chapter on Degeneration is a good sermon from the text of the Sluggard's Garden in Solomon's Proverbs;[1] but its scientific value is null, in view of the fact that the weeds which overgrow such a garden, and the wild types to which domesticated races of plants and animals revert when neglected, are not, from a biological point of view, degenerate races at all.

In the chapter on Environment, however, he gets much nearer to spiritual realities. It is a well-reasoned and eloquent plea, from the facts of the world of nature, for that doctrine of our absolute dependence on God which is fundamental in every religion that deserves the name of a religion at all. We have always known that we are dependent on our physical environment—on the world around us —for the food we eat and the air we breathe. Science has now added to this, the proof that we are equally dependent on it for our supply of force —that the will can no more create force, either muscular or mental, than it can create matter. And it is equally true that for our spiritual nourishment and spiritual force we are altogether dependent on our spiritual environment, which is God. It is well to have on this subject a clearly-stated and

[1] Proverbs xxiv. 30.

forcible argument, which, though not in principle new, yet looks new in its new scientific setting; but it is wonderful that such proofs and illustrations should ever have been needed—that man should ever have thought it possible to be self-sufficing. And, as has been remarked by one of the profoundest of religious thinkers, Erskine of Linlathen,[1] "there is nothing degrading in this dependence, for we share it with the Eternal Son"; it is not a consequence of sin or of any tendency thereto.

[1] *The Spiritual Order and other Papers, selected from the MSS. of Thomas Erskine of Linlathen.* P. 233. Edmonston and Douglas, 1871.

CHAPTER II.

REGENERATION.

In the foregoing chapter, we have been only on the ground of Nature and what is called Natural Religion. We have now to consider the subject of Divine Revelation and Divine Grace, and to examine Professor Drummond's most important and most characteristic doctrine, which he calls Spiritual Biogenesis.

Biogenesis is defined as the generation of life from life only. We have every reason to believe that this is an absolute law of the natural world —that every living thing, vegetable or animal, is descended from living parents, and that the origin of life was as much a direct act of Creative Power as the origin of matter. Tyndall's celebrated saying, that matter contains the "promise and potency of life," is not supported by experimental evidence, and indeed it has been propounded by its author only as an effort of imaginative faith. But, so far as experiment can prove a negative, it proves that mere matter does not contain any *potency* of life: it has only a *capacity* of being vitalised by previously existing life. And it certainly contains no promise of life; for the profoundest knowledge of the physical and chemical properties of matter would not give the faintest hint or suggestion of life.[1]

Now, according to Professor Drummond, the very same law — that life can be produced only from life—is true also in the spiritual world; and its expression in the spiritual world is the law of Regeneration: that, as matter can become living only by the agency of already existing life, so mind can acquire spiritual life only through the agency of the Divine Spirit. This is according to Christ's saying, "Ye must be born anew," as reported by Saint John in that conversation with Nicodemus which has become the classical passage on the doctrine of Regeneration;[2] and, in the classical passage on the doctrine of the Resurrection, Saint Paul says the same in different words: "The first man is of the earth, earthy: the second man is of heaven. . . . And as we have borne the image of the earthy, we shall also bear the image of the heavenly."[3]

No doctrine is more profoundly true, and with none does fanaticism more easily ally itself. But

---

[1] Huxley says: "The present state of knowledge furnishes us with no link between the living and the not living." And Virchow speaks of the theory of spontaneous, or "equivocal," generation as "utterly discredited." (Quoted by Drummond, p. 70, note.)

[2] John iii. 7, Revised Version.   [3] 1 Cor. xv. 47, 49.

though Professor Drummond's analogy between natural and spiritual Biogenesis is impressive and instructive, it is by no means a close analogy; yet his special claim is to establish not analogies but identities of law. The analogy between the weed or the worm deriving natural life from its own ancestors, and man deriving spiritual life from the Divine Source of all life, however real, is certainly but remote: it is one of those analogies of which nature is full, which hold good only to a certain extent and in certain relations. In applying this analogy, moreover, Professor Drummond appears to have been led into inaccuracy of thought by confounding two senses of the word Death. Its proper meaning is the state of that which has been living, and is so no longer. But it is also used in the sense of merely lifeless: in this sense we speak of "mere dead matter." Now, this secondary sense of the word ought to have no place in a scientific treatise. It would be inaccurate to use the word immoral as a synonym of not moral, and to call the love of life an immoral agency because it does not belong to the moral nature; and the inaccuracy is as great when Professor Drummond uses, as he constantly does, the same word, death, for the state of a soul which is "dead in trespasses and sins," and for the state of a soul which is not spiritually living only because it has not yet been breathed upon by the Life-giving Spirit. In the former case, sin, *being full-grown*, has brought forth its legitimate offspring, which is death;[1] the latter is the state of childlike innocence, like that of Adam and Eve in the allegorical tradition which until our own time was mistaken for history, who had not committed sin, and yet, not having eaten the fruit of the tree of life,[2] were in a merely natural and not in a spiritual state. Disease, death, and corruption are the appropriate symbols of sin. The state of the natural soul, not yet born anew of the Spirit of God, may no doubt be fitly symbolised by matter which is not living; but such matter may be of crystalline purity; and though a crystal is not living, it is in no true sense dead. Yet the whole of Professor Drummond's work is obscured by this confusion. Spiritual Biogenesis, or the derivation of spiritual life in man solely from the Divine Source of all life, is, however, his characteristic doctrine: and we go on to inquire in what sense it is true. I do not ask whether it *is* true; for every one who believes in a spiritual cosmos at all, however vaguely, must believe that God is the source of all life[3] and the "Father of Spirits."[4]

He maintains that the spiritual man is contrasted with the natural man, as a living organism with unvitalised matter; and that the natural and unregenerate soul is to the Spirit of God in the same relation as mere matter to the vital powers. Now this, like most analogies and parables, may

---

[1] James i. 15, Revised Version.　　[2] Genesis iii. 22.
[3] Psalm civ. 30.　　[4] Hebrews xii. 9.

easily be so pressed as to become inconsistent with fact. Were it true in any complete and absolute sense, it would imply that the human faculties of reverence, love, and worship first came into existence when the gift of the Holy Spirit was first imparted to men; and that these have no existence at all in unspiritual men, but are created at the critical moment of regeneration (or, as Professor Drummond always calls it, conversion). But this is contrary to the most obvious fact. And, moreover, the language of Christ and of His Prophets and Apostles assumes the contrary: it assumes that the powers of spiritual discernment, knowledge, and love are naturally present in man, and waiting to be rightly directed. "The isles shall wait for (the revelation of) His law,"[1] said Isaiah; Christ said, in the act of revealing Himself to Saul the persecutor, "It is hard for thee to kick against the goad"[2] (of conscience); and after the persecutor had become an Apostle, he said to the idolaters of Athens, "The unknown God, whom ye worship in ignorance, Him I declare unto you."[3] These are but a few instances of the appeals addressed by God and His messengers to the natural reason, the natural conscience, and the natural heart — an appeal which would have no meaning if the natural man were but as lifeless matter in relation to the Spirit of God.

We ought not to forget that God, even in the darkest ages, has "left Himself not without witness,"

---

[1] Isaiah xlii. 4.   [2] Acts xxvi. 14.   [3] Acts xvii. 23.

not only in sending "rain and fruitful seasons,"[1] but in men's hearts and consciences, however perverted. Were it not so, we should have no means whatever of attracting the irreligious and the heathen to Divine truth: we could not proclaim a message to the conscience of men, if it were impossible to express the message in a language which their conscience could understand. Any successful call on men to believe, must appeal to their latent capacity for faith, and their half-felt need of a Divine Saviour. To quote from one of the most beautiful of our hymns—

> Far and wide, though all unknowing,
>   Pants for Thee each mortal breast;
> Human tears for Thee are flowing,
>   Human hearts in Thee would rest.
>
> Thirsting as for dews of even,
>   As the new-mown grass for rain,
> Thee they seek as God of Heaven,
>   Thee as Man for sinners slain.
>
> Saviour, lo! the isles are waiting!
>   Stretched the hand and strained the sight,
> For Thy Spirit new-creating,
>   Love's pure flame and wisdom's light![2]

Drummond ignores this. If he were consistent with himself—which, as we shall see farther on, he is not—he must deny any such blind presentiment, in the natural man, of the revelation to be made; and for means to produce conviction of the

---

[1] Acts xiv. 17.   [2] Bishop Coxe.

truth of the revelation, he must rely exclusively on those historical evidences which with the instructed have much less power than they deserve, and with the uninstructed appear to have no power whatever.

But this does not close the subject. There is another analogy to the relation between the Spirit of God and the soul of man, which, though less rhetorically effective than Professor Drummond's, is far more profoundly true. The merely natural man is analogous, not to dead or unvitalised matter, but to a living though undeveloped organism; and the regenerating agency of the Spirit of God in the human soul is most fitly symbolised by the agency of the Organising Intelligence which guides the evolution of living beings.

The doctrine of organic Evolution may now be regarded as unquestionable, and Professor Drummond fully accepts it. But evolution is not necessarily self-evolution, and an evolutionist is not necessarily a Darwinian. Just as I believe, with Professor Drummond, that God's Holy Spirit alone can impart spiritual life, so I believe that only a Creative and Organising Intelligence can originate and direct the formative agencies of organic life. In my opinion, the attempt of Darwin and Herbert Spencer to explain away the "argument from design" has totally failed, and the necessity of recognising a Creative Intelligence, working towards a Purpose, is as strong now as it appeared to be in Paley's time.

For the development of the great vertebrate class out of the lowly, worm-like, and undeveloped Ascidian larva, of the bird out of the reptile, and above all, of the man out of an ape-like form, an Intelligent Power is needed, transcending all the powers, not only of unvitalised matter, but of the unintelligent life of mere habit and hereditary transmission.

When an organ has to be adapted to a new function, or an organism to a new mode of life—it may be to a new element, as when a water-breathing larva turns into an air-breathing perfect form—the usual method of the Organising Intelligence is not to call a new organ into existence, but to adapt one already existing. Thus, the lungs of air-breathing vertebrates are beyond doubt a modification of the swim-bladder of fishes; the wing of the bird is a modification of the fore-leg of the reptile; and the wings of insects have most probably been formed by the modification of organs for aquatic respiration. So it is in the process whereby the Spirit of God transforms the natural into the spiritual man. The powers of reverence, knowledge, and love are not conferred for the first time, but they receive a new direction; they were formerly directed to earthly, probably unworthy, certainly inadequate and unsatisfying, objects; now they are directed to the only perfectly worthy, adequate, and satisfying Object. This view of the true natural analogue of spiritual regeneration is, no doubt, unfamiliar, and may perhaps appear startling; but it is not more so than Professor Drummond's doctrine which we have been considering; and the Psalmist long ago spoke of the Spirit of God as the source of merely natural life.[1]

It may be thought that this question, arising out of what looks like mere poetical symbolism, cannot be of any real importance. But this is not so. What we are considering is nothing less than the entire subject of the relation between Nature and Grace; and speculative errors on such a subject may be practically injurious. I have already remarked, that the first effect of Drummond's theory on this subject — if it were heartily accepted, which, however, is scarcely to be feared — would be to deprive believers of any means of reaching the minds of doubters and unbelievers. Professor Drummond appears not only to accept but to emphasise this consequence. He says: "The endeavours of well-meaning persons to show that the agnostic's position, when he asserts his ignorance of the spiritual world, is only a pretence; the attempts to prove that he really knows a great deal about it if he would only admit it, are quite misplaced. He really does not know. The verdict that the natural man receiveth not the things of the Spirit of God, that they are foolishness unto him, that *neither can he*

---

[1] Psalm civ. 30. For the view stated in the foregoing paragraph, the writer is indebted to the article in the *British Quarterly Review* of July 1884, entitled "Evolution viewed in relation to Theology," being a review of the second edition of the present writer's work, *Habit and Intelligence* (Macmillan, 1879).

know them, is final as a statement of scientific truth —a statement on which the entire agnostic literature is one long commentary." [1]

Any admission whatever ought no doubt to be made if its truth is proved beyond question. But so tremendous an admission ought not to be made without almost lifelong consideration; yet Professor Drummond has made it in the heat of controversy, in a work which bears many marks of somewhat hasty composition, and apparently without perceiving that it is an admission at all. Yet it amounts to asserting in sober earnest what David Hume said with a sneer—I quote from memory— that Christianity is so miraculous, it takes a miracle to make a man believe it. This saying of Drummond's amounts to admitting that the sceptic and the agnostic are right from their own point of view —that the power of recognising, believing, and knowing spiritual truth is not an endowment of the race of man, but is specially and miraculously conferred on a few, who have no means of making its existence known to those who are without it; that the only message of the Christian preacher and the Christian missionary to the ignorant masses of mankind is, "I have a Gospel to proclaim, but you have no faculty whereby to understand it."

It is, no doubt, Saint Paul who says that "the natural man receiveth not the things of the Spirit of God; and he cannot know them, because

[1] *Natural Law in the Spiritual World*, p. 78.

they are spiritually discerned."[1] But a writer who is endeavouring to throw the light of science on the things of faith ought not to quote such a statement as "final," in the sense of finally decisive of such a question, without inquiring in what sense the words are used; whether their most obvious sense is their deepest sense; and whether some meaning has not been read into them which may not be their own. These words assert that natural things and spiritual things are to be apprehended by different faculties; but they say nothing of the nature or source of those faculties. The relation between them may, however, be thus illustrated:—If a man totally ignorant of both mathematical and experimental methods, were for the first time told of the most remarkable results of science, such as the motion of the earth, the theory of luminous undulations, or the perhaps yet more wonderful discovery of the atomic constitution of matter, he would probably reply: "Not only I see no evidence for the truth of this, but I cannot imagine any such evidence to exist." To which the answer would be, "Certainly you do not and cannot see it. Before you can see it, you must acquire what will be in effect new faculties. The merely perceptive intellect receives not the things of science, neither can it know them, because they are scientifically discerned." Now, as the scientific faculty is a development of the ordinary understanding, so is the

[1] 1 Cor. ii. 14.

spiritual faculty a development from germs which have always existed in the natural instincts of man.

Professor Drummond is not unaware of this. He says: "The chamber is not only ready to receive the new life, but the Guest is expected, and till He comes is missed. Till then the soul longs and yearns, wastes and pines, feeling after God, if so be that it may find Him. In every land and in every age there have been altars to the known or unknown God. It is now agreed, as a mere question of anthropology, that the universal language of the human soul has always been, 'I perish with hunger.' This is what fits it for Christ. There is a grandeur in this cry from the depths which makes its very unhappiness sublime."[1] This is true, and most forcibly and admirably said, but it appears quite inconsistent with all the rest of the book. Unvitalised matter, to which, as we have seen, he elsewhere compares the unregenerate soul, does not long for life or aspire after it.

To a being watching the evolution of worlds from without, Life would seem altogether new. Let us imagine a spirit dwelling in space, with vision at once telescopic and microscopic, watching the evolution of worlds by the condensation of a nebula, "the gathering together of waters to form seas" on the surface of the planets, the channelling of their river-beds and the flow of their rivers, their currents

---

[1] *Natural Law in the Spiritual World*, p. 300.

of air and of ocean, their clouds, their storms, their glaciers, their volcanoes, their formation of rock-strata and of mineral veins. If he had knowledge of the properties of matter like ours in kind but much wider and deeper, every stage in the process of this evolution would appear the natural and necessary consequence of that next before it. But when life made its appearance, this would be no longer so: here, for the first time, would be something explicable neither by the inherent properties of matter, nor by the preceding steps of the evolutionary process; but a new creation, totally unlike anything that had appeared before, and not suggested by it.

To such a being, man's nature would become intelligible only when spiritual life was awakened. Let us further suppose him to watch the evolution of the organic world, and note the ways and the instincts of animals; and further, not only to see but to understand man as the wisest men understand themselves: would he regard man as merely an animal, distinguished from other animals chiefly by the possession of language, and the power to invent and use tools and machinery; and having some strange and unaccountable ways, of which the strangest was that of inventing deities and worshipping them? And when spiritual life was awakened by the Spirit of God in some favoured individuals, would this spiritual life, like organic life on its first appearance, seem not only a new creation, but something not even suggested by the world in the midst of which it appeared? Surely the relation of the spiritual to the natural life is very different from this. So far from coming as a surprise to the supposed angelic observer, the wonder would be that it had not come long before. The coming of Christ into the world, with the gift of the Holy Spirit and the promise of eternal life, would be seen to reveal the meaning of that wonderful human instinct of worship, and to provide, for the first time, a perfectly worthy Object for the human powers of reverence and love.

Drummond's theory of Regeneration raises this further difficulty :—If it is true, as he teaches, that spiritual life is not conferred on the race of man by creation, but only on a chosen few by conversion, how can we resist the conclusion that resurrection and a future life are for the just alone, and that the unjust perish like the beasts? In reply to this he rejects such an inference with a mere protest. At the end of a most eloquent and true exposition of the nature and meaning of judgment, showing that it is in no degree arbitrary, but is the natural and necessary consequence of sin, he goes on to say—"Should any one object that from this scientific standpoint the opposite of salvation is annihilation, the answer is at hand. From this standpoint there is no such word."[1] Why not? Does he mean that

---

[1] *Natural Law in the Spiritual World*, p. 117.

there is a scientifically-proved law of the conservation of consciousness through death, analogous to the law of the conservation of force (or, more accurately, energy) through its transformations? He is a scientific man, and must be aware that no such law has been, or possibly can be, established : yet if not, what does his argument mean? The fact is that he teaches, throughout, the doctrine of immortality for those alone who are converted to God, and protects himself and his readers against the obvious inference from this doctrine by a feeble, illogical, and almost unmeaning protest. The obvious inference must be that there is practically no future judgment—that if a man chooses to be a beast, he will no more come into judgment than a beast. This would, no doubt, in one way be a welcome relief from the horrible thought of conscious spirits being condemned to remain with the burden of their sins through all eternity, without any possibility of either salvation from without or conversion from within. But to announce to men that they need not come into judgment unless they please, would be, for those who should accept it, to abolish the restraint of law : and all theory and all experience agree in teaching that without a Law of Righteousness to build on, there can be no Gospel of Salvation. The doctrine of no judgment, and the doctrine of the hopelessness of the future state, are alike opposed to the true doctrine of the Prophets and Apostles and of Christ Himself, namely, that there shall be a "restoration of all things,"[1] when all enemies shall be abolished, and God shall be all in all.[2] I shall have to speak at fuller length on this subject in the chapter on the Final Destiny of the Rejected.

I deny, as emphatically as Professor Drummond, that regeneration is a merely natural process. Spiritual life is not merely natural, just as organic life is not merely physical and chemical. There are, as he has shown, three kingdoms, or Divine administrations, not excluding each other, but as it were successively superimposed. First is the inorganic kingdom, or that of mere matter and force. Second, the organic kingdom, or that of Life, having its highest development in the mind of man. These two together constitute the world of nature as opposed to the spiritual world. Above these is the spiritual kingdom, which is related to that of nature as the organic world to the inorganic. All these, though not equally near to God, are alike His creation; and—although Professor Drummond does not remark this—God has chiefly manifested His might in the inorganic kingdom, His intelligence in the organic, and His moral nature—His holiness and His love—in the spiritual.

[1] Acts iii. 21.   [2] 1 Cor. xv. 24, 28.

CHAPTER III.

CONVERSION.

"WE must be born anew." "As we have borne the image of the earthy, we shall also bear the image of the heavenly, even of the Lord from heaven." Such is the teaching of Divine Wisdom as to the necessity of Regeneration. The meaning of this has been considered in the foregoing chapter; and it is now time to ask the question, What do Professor Drummond, and the entire school of thought to which he belongs, mean by habitually using the word Conversion in place of Regeneration?

The most obvious reply is that the words are synonymously used in the teaching of Christ: that the saying to the disciples, "Except ye be converted and become as little children, ye shall in no wise enter the kingdom of heaven,"[1] is a mere repetition of the saying to Nicodemus, "Except a man be born of water and of the Spirit, he cannot enter into the kingdom of God." But there are many reasons why this view is untenable. In the first place, it

[1] Matt. xviii. 3.

is very seldom that any two words are perfectly synonymous; and if, in quotation, we substitute one expression for another that comes near it in meaning, there may be a danger of doing injustice to its intention.

In the second place, the two sayings that we have quoted were spoken on very different occasions. That to Nicodemus was formal, general, dogmatic teaching; that to the disciples, on the contrary, arose out of an occasion of the moment. They had been asking, "Who is greatest in the kingdom of heaven?" meaning only, "Which of us shall be Thy chief minister when we have got rid of the Romans and of Herod, and Thou art seated on the throne of David and Solomon?" and He refused to give an answer, but intimated that their question was framed in a wrong spirit, and that He demands a childlike temper in those who would follow Him. These words are, no doubt, for all time, but it is not the less true that their full significance depends on the circumstances under which they were spoken.

In the third place, the expression *to be converted* is not grammatically accurate. The Greek verb which in the Authorised Version is so translated, is not in the passive but in the middle voice, and the Revised Version, with its accustomed careful accuracy, has everywhere substituted *to turn*.[1]

---

[1] But though it is never used with this meaning in the passive voice, it is once so used in the active, namely, in James v. 19, 20; and in that passage the Revisers have retained the translation "convert."

To this it may perhaps be answered: "The change in the Revised Version from the passive to the middle—substituting *to turn* for *to be turned*—is exactly what was needed to show the distinction between regeneration and conversion. Regeneration is the word chosen to express the part of God in the work of grace: God is the Father of Spirits, *who, according to His great mercy, begat us again unto a living hope, by the resurrection of Jesus Christ from the dead.*[1] Conversion, or turning, is the word that expresses man's part: the Holy Spirit demands our co-operation in the work." I reply, that this does not correctly explain Our Lord's use of the expression *conversion*, or *turning*. When the Apostles were going to be immediately exposed to a severer trial than any they had yet dreamed of, and when He knew that Peter's faith would fail for the moment, He said: "Simon, Simon, Satan hath desired to have you, that he may sift you as wheat: but I have prayed for thee, that thy faith fail not: and when thou art converted, strengthen thy brethren."[2] So in the Authorised Version; but for "when thou art converted," the Revised Version substitutes "when once thou hast turned again." The change is most significant. Christ foresaw that Peter, under the pressure of overwhelming fear, would commit that sin of denying his Lord, which, from his position as chief of the Apostles and from the dramatic character

---

[1] 1 Peter i. 3.   [2] Luke xxii. 31, 32.

of the incident, has greatly impressed the imagination of men; though in the light of eternity it was probably less than the smallest sin of calculation. He accordingly gave Peter an affectionate warning, with a promise that he should be sustained; addressing him, not as though he were outside the kingdom of God and needed to be brought into it, but as a soldier already enlisted in the service of the King, and beginning an arduous and dangerous warfare in that service. This is sufficiently shown by Christ's words, "I have prayed for thee, that thy faith fail not"; implying that he had faith already. And the Apostle must have been already regenerate and brought into the kingdom, when he was one of the three who were permitted to behold the heavenly glory of the Christ on Mount Hermon; and when, in answer to his declaration, "Thou art the Christ, the Son of the living God," he received the testimony, "Blessed art thou, Simon son of Jonah: for flesh and blood (*i.e.* the natural understanding) hath not revealed it unto thee, but My Father which is in heaven."[1] This appears to be conclusive proof that in Christ's view it may be necessary and possible for a man to "turn again" after he has been "born anew" and received into the kingdom of God. And if so, to "turn again," or, in the Authorised Version, to "be converted," is not a synonymous expression for to be "born anew."

Now, we have seen that Professor Drummond

[1] Matt. xvi. 17.

constantly uses the word conversion instead of regeneration, and that (except in one passage where for a moment he half-unconsciously deviates into a deeper truth), he defines conversion as the result of an action of the Spirit of God on a soul which in relation to that Spirit was but as dead matter. Let us compare this view of regeneration with mine as set forth in the foregoing chapter. The legitimate consequence of Professor Drummond's theory of conversion appears to be this: That as matter contains no potency or promise of life, it is not responsible for being without life (or dead, to use his misleading word); and if it is ever to live, it must wait for the life-giving influence to come unsought; so, the human soul, having no promise or potency of spiritual life in itself, is not responsible for being spiritually dead, and cannot seek for life, but must passively wait for the Spirit of God to come unsought; and may in the meantime make the best of this present world without taking thought of any other. If the natural man has no spiritual nature whatever, and consequently no spiritual privileges which he can abuse, how can he be held blameworthy for being unspiritual? Further, What is the position of young children in the spiritual world? Professor Drummond appears to teach that conversion is a process which necessarily occurs in consciousness; he does not expressly lay this down, but he seems everywhere to imply it; and the doctrine of "the necessity of conversion" appears to be generally held in this sense, though in an undecided sort of way, by those who belong to the same school of religious thought with him. Now, if a human being can become spiritual, and capable of eternal life, only by conversion occurring within consciousness, what is to become of those who pass out of the present life before religious consciousness has been awakened? If Professor Drummond's theory were true, the position of infants in relation to spiritual life would be analogous to the position of matter in relation to natural life in the ages before life was introduced into the world of matter; and the inference from this would be that they cannot attain to eternal life—not perhaps sharing the fate of devils, but at least that of beasts. Conscience, however, rejects this: the belief in infant salvation is almost universal, and I have no doubt Professor Drummond shares it. But if any believe—as thousands do, or fancy they do—at once in the salvation of infants unto eternal life, and in the necessity of conscious conversion occurring at a definite time, they are sounder in their instinct than in their logic.

The reply to this will probably be that the case of young children in the eternal world is exceptional; but Christ declares that it is normal. "Except ye become as little children," He says, "ye shall in no wise enter into the kingdom of heaven." This leads on to a question which is of the highest practical importance, and is far too seldom distinctly asked. How are children in the enjoyment of Christian

privileges to be regarded ? Our Lord has said :—
"Their angels always behold the face of My Father
which is in heaven";[1] and Saint Paul says to
Christian parents, "Your children are holy."[2] Is it
possible to rest in the conclusion that every infant
has an inheritance in heaven, but that when it grows
old enough to be conscious of the difference between
good and evil, and, like all human beings, to fall into
sin, it must be treated as a child of the devil until
it is consciously converted ? Is it to be given up as
impossible for any to walk from the cradle to the
grave without at some time losing their baptismal
purity ? Must Christian parents teach their children,
not only that they have tendencies to sin, with which
all are born, and that they sometimes fall into actual
sin, from which none altogether escape ; but that it
is a necessity of our nature, not to be avoided even
by the grace of God through the Lord Jesus Christ,
that baptismal purity must be lost, and that some
part of every life which is prolonged beyond early
childhood must be passed in alienation from God ?
Is the returned Prodigal the type of every true
Christian ? Most, perhaps, would dread to assert this
as a dogma ; if they did, the proper result would be
what I have been credibly informed that a mother
actually said :—" My children are not converted, and
if I were to teach them the Lord's Prayer I must
teach them to say *Our Father which art in hell.*" Few
would express themselves with such brutal directness ;

[1] Matt. xviii. 10.   [2] 1 Cor. vii. 14.

but it seems to be really implied, though probably not intended, in much that is said about the necessity for conversion. It is, I fear, true that the greater part of most of the congregations which the preacher addresses do need conversion, and need to be reminded of the need. But the doctrine of the necessity of conversion becomes false if it is so stated as to deny that any can hope to walk, like Samuel under the old covenant and Timothy under the new, from the cradle to the grave in the light of God.

Such a denial is dangerous to the Christian life in two different ways. With some dispositions the inference will be, "If by the terms of the case we must be sinners, let us at least enjoy the pleasures of sin for a season"; and thus the doctrine of regeneration and conversion will be perverted into a sanction of the worst falsehood of a corrupt world, which teaches that what are euphemistically called the errors of youth are inevitable, and to be thought of with little more horror and dread than the diseases of childhood. Those who have sinned under such influences have often, I doubt not, been converted afterwards, and enabled truly to serve God; though it may be doubted whether purity of heart, when so lost, is ever perfectly recovered in the present life. But there are others with whom perverted teaching on this subject leaves the soul's purity untouched, but hinders and mars the legitimate effect of purity—namely, peace, joy, and happiness. And loss of peace entails, moreover, loss of power to serve God and man. We need

> A heart at leisure from itself,
> To soothe and sympathise.

If biography tells little of the injury due by such causes, this is because those who suffer from them longest and most deeply are the least inclined to make their injuries and sufferings known : it is inevitable, and not on the whole to be regretted, that in general the successes of every system of religious education should be recorded, and its failures forgotten. Evidence on this subject is, however, to be found. One instance is afforded in the life of that sweet singer and noble-minded woman Frances Ridley Havergal.[1] We are told in the autobiographical fragment published in her Memoirs, that from the age of six to that of fourteen she suffered from religious fears, and did not venture to call herself a Christian ; and yet she appears to have been through her whole life one of those who are clean, and need not save to wash their feet.[2] So far as a reader of her life and writings can judge, the sufferings of that pure and spiritually aspiring child were totally needless, and due to erroneous teaching respecting the kingdom of Him who desires His

---

[1] She says in a letter to a friend : "I am unable to fix the date of my conversion." Most probably it was never needed, and never occurred at all. I say this, knowing that she would have regarded it as heresy.

[2] John xiii. 10.

subjects to be like little children. It is altogether contrary to fact, to teach that every true child of God not only is at peace with Him, but consciously possesses and enjoys such peace.[1] She came out of the trial, so far as her Memoirs show, without the smell of fire on her garments; but it is not so with all— it was not so with the mother of Professor Maurice, who is described in her son's *Life* as an admirable and deeply religious woman, who yet endured long and deep mental suffering from doubts as to her own "personal election."

The doctrine here insisted on, as to the rightful position of the children of Christians, is that implied in the phrase Baptismal Regeneration. I do not altogether like the phrase, but perhaps this is only because it has been fought over in the Church of Ireland until it has become to most persons a mere catchword. The principle implied in it is, however, the truth that every child of Christian parents who is placed in possession of Christian privileges is "holy" and "grafted into the body of Christ's Church"; and that the ideal and the aim of Christian education ought to be, not that this purity shall be regained in future years after being lost, but that it may never be lost at all. And we may thankfully

---

[1] "Being justified by faith, we have (ἔχομεν) peace with God," says St. Paul (Rom. v. i.) So in the Authorised Version; but the Revised adopts the reading ἔχωμεν, and translates "let us have peace." The Apostle does not assert that all sincere believers actually enjoy such peace; what he means is, "Let us enter into that peace which is our right."

acknowledge that some among us prove the attainableness of this ideal by attaining it—that there are at least some men, and many women, who serve God and walk in His light from the cradle to the grave without any period of alienation from Him.

The following is a summary of the conclusions to which we have reached in the foregoing and the present chapters:—

Man, in his merely natural and unregenerate state, has nevertheless spiritual faculties, to which, in the regenerate, the Holy Spirit gives direction and development; and the most appropriate natural symbol of regeneration is not the vitalisation of dead matter, but the action of Creative Intelligence in guiding vital evolution. As in vital evolution an organ becomes adapted to a new function, and an organism to new surroundings, so in spiritual regeneration the heart and mind are set on new objects, and become adapted to the spiritual world.

This view of the nature of regeneration makes intelligible and conceivable—what is, moreover, a fact of experience—that it should be possible to walk from the cradle to the grave, not indeed altogether without sin, but without any period of alienation from God, and with the heavenly life developing along with the earthly, as it did in Christ, from the first. The school of religious thought which Professor Drummond so ably represents, by habitually using the word Conversion instead of

Regeneration, appear to ignore the possibility of such a life, and to teach that every true child of God must have become so by returning to Him after wandering away. By speaking in preference of Regeneration, I on the contrary indicate my belief that such conversion ought not to be, and is not always, needed: that the typical Christian is he who has served Christ from his earliest years; who has never lost his baptismal purity, but, being clean, has only to wash his feet of their daily stains.[1]

In the following chapter we shall consider what Christ teaches respecting the possibility of such a life of unbroken, though not perfect, service of God from the beginning.

[1] John xiii. 10.

CHAPTER IV.

TWO OF CHRIST'S PARABLES.

[This chapter is a reproduction of "The Elder Brother of the Prodigal," in the *Monthly Interpreter*, 1885; and "Two Parables," in the *Expositor* of April 1889; both by the present writer.]

THERE is but little resemblance between the external form and imagery of the parable of the Prodigal Son [1] and that of the Labourers in the Vineyard,[2] except that both are taken from the relations of men in common life; and they were spoken on very different occasions. The parable of the Prodigal, which was the earlier of the two, was mainly addressed to the Pharisees, in reply to their complaint against Jesus that "this man receiveth sinners and eateth with them." The parable of the Labourers in the Vineyard was spoken to the disciples alone, in reply to Peter's question, when, after the young ruler had shown himself unable to give up all for Christ, he said on behalf of the twelve, "Lo, we have forsaken all and followed Thee; what shall we have therefore?"

[1] Luke xv. 11, 32.   [2] Matt. xix. 27; xx. 16.

The parable of the Prodigal has probably impressed mankind more than anything else in Christ's teaching, and in its most impressive feature is perfectly clear; while that of the Labourers has impressed mankind comparatively little, and appears to be generally thought a perplexing parable. Nevertheless it can be shown that the lessons of the two are closely similar.

The lesson of both parables is twofold. In the one we have the cases of the two sons, in the other those of the first hired and the last hired labourers; and in both, equal emphasis is laid on the two cases; though this is not generally seen. It is perhaps for this reason to be regretted that the former has received the name of the parable of the Prodigal Son: it would be better to call it the parable of the Two Sons, were not this title already appropriated to another parable, also spoken to the Pharisees and rulers.[1]

The three parables in Luke xv., the Lost Sheep, the Lost Piece of Money, and the Lost Son, or the Prodigal, were evidently spoken about the same time, and form a series. But the words "and He said," at the commencement of the third, indicate a transition of some kind; and perhaps Our Lord, at this point of His discourse, meant, and was understood by His audience to mean, "I have till now been addressing the Pharisees in defence of my action in receiving sinners and eating

[1] Matt. xxi. 28.

with them. I have yet more to say on the action of God and His Son in seeking and saving the lost; and to this I demand the attention equally of the righteous and of sinners, of Pharisees and of publicans."

Probably nothing else that Christ has taught has been so well learned by His Church as the lessons of these parables, that repentance is possible even after a career of open sin; that it will be accepted by God, and ought to be accepted by man. On the contrary, it was by this feature of Our Lord's life and teaching that the religious men of the Jewish Church—the Pharisees—were most offended. They called Him—truly, though not in the sense which they intended—a friend of sinners; they really believed Him to be a subverter of moral distinctions. Yet they might have learned better from the prophets whose sepulchres they built and adorned. Isaiah had written long before, "Wash you, make you clean; put away the evil of your doings from before mine eyes. . . . Though your sins be as scarlet, they shall be as white as snow: though they be red like crimson, they shall be as wool."[1] No language of Christ's could be stronger. But this, like many other prophetic sayings, appears to have remained unappreciated and uncomprehended until it was adopted into the teaching of Christ.

There is no room for doubt or controversy as to the meaning of that part of the parable which tells of

[1] Isaiah i. 16, 18.

the Prodigal himself. The story of his sins and his misfortunes is repeated in every age and in every country; and to those who heard, whether Pharisees or publicans, he represented the "sinners," by receiving and eating with whom Christ scandalised the Pharisees. But what are we to make of the elder brother, who had remained at home with his father all the time of the Prodigal's absence; and when the Prodigal returned, and was received by his father with honour and festivity, was so angry and sullen that he would not enter the house?

It is not likely the Pharisees had any difficulty in perceiving that Christ meant this as a condemnation of their position. But to many modern readers it seems to be perplexing: they probably think the conversation where the father justifies himself to his elder son for receiving the returned prodigal with rejoicing, is meant only to heighten the effect of the whole. If, however, we were now to read it for the first time, it would not heighten the effect; and it may be suspected that those who think so, would in reality like the parable better if it ended with the reception of the Prodigal by the father.

There is, no doubt, a difficulty about the way in which we are to understand the character of the elder brother. He is usually taken to represent the Pharisees, and he appears to be introduced solely for rebuke and warning; yet the father's saying, "Son, thou art ever with me, and all that is mine is thine," describes a state of privilege and blessing equal to the highest that any created being can hope to attain. Compare Saint Paul's assertions of the blessedness of God's children: "If children, then heirs: heirs of God, and joint heirs with Christ."[1] "Whether the world, or life, or death, or things present, or things to come, all are yours."[2] The apparent inconsistency may, however, be easily reconciled. Our Lord in this parable chose, for the sake of argument and illustration, to take the Pharisees at their best, and to describe not the actual but the ideal Pharisee—one who, like Saint Paul before his conversion to Christ, was neither covetous, nor unjust, nor impure, but "as touching the righteousness which is in the law, found blameless."[3] This, it is true, was far short of the Christian ideal, for "the law was given by Moses, but grace and truth came by Jesus Christ";[4] but it was the ideal of righteousness held up to ancient Israel; and He so framed the parable as to show them the special errors and temptations of such a character—of those who, like the elder son, have never left the Father's house, and therefore have never had to return to it; who have never needed to pass through a crisis of conversion, but, like Samuel in the Old Testament and Timothy in the New, have from childhood been so instructed as to be made wise unto salvation; whose blessedness is that godliness is with them a habit, while their danger is that it may be nothing more.

[1] Romans viii. 17. [2] 1 Cor. iii. 22.
[3] Philippians iii. 6. [4] John i. 17.

The characteristic danger of such a life and such a character is a narrowness of mind which tends to set the observance of a Sabbath, or other piece of ceremonial, on an equality with justice, mercy, and purity; and it belongs to the same legal and somewhat mechanical view of righteousness, that the elder son found it difficult to believe in the possibility of repentance, and impossible to believe that a repentant sinner ought to be, at once and completely, restored to the position of a child. And this mechanical view of righteousness and narrowness of sympathy, though it did not alienate him from his father, yet made his service of his father less filial and less happy than it ought to have been. His unsympathising and unpitying harshness to the returning Prodigal is what strikes us most—and this is what Our Lord intended. But let us not be unjust to him. Harshness to a returning prodigal was by no means so manifestly contrary to the will of God under the old dispensation as it has been since Our Lord spoke this wonderful parable; and, deeply as its lesson has sunk into the mind of Christendom, yet perhaps the commonest feeling, even of good men, on this subject is still that of the people described by an English novelist, with whom repentant prodigals "were sure of their daily bread, but it had to be eaten with the proper quantity of bitter herbs."[1] What was worst in the elder son was not his unbrotherly feeling towards his brother,

---

[1] *The Mill on the Floss,* by George Eliot.

for which there was much provocation and excuse, but his unfilial feeling towards his father, for which there was none. He was no doubt a true and obedient son: his boast, "I never transgressed a commandment of thine," remained uncontradicted, and was evidently true. But from our Christian point of view the question must arise, How is this possible? How can any man say that he never transgressed a commandment of his heavenly Father? As the wise king said, "Who can say, I have made my heart clean, I am pure from my sin?"[1] or, as the same thought has been expanded by Matthew Arnold—

>   What mortal, when he saw,
>   Life's voyage done, his Heavenly Friend,
>   Could ever yet dare tell Him fearlessly:—
>   I have kept uninfringed my nature's law:
>   The inly written chart Thou gavest me
>   To guide me, I have kept by to the end?

The difficulty, however, disappears if we are satisfied to use words in a way that is sanctioned by Scripture, and not to insist on the most definite theological sense of every word. What is meant is not perfect obedience, for this is attained by none, but constant habitual obedience, which is attained by many. The apostle who says, "If we say that we have no sin, we deceive ourselves," says a little farther on, "Whosoever abideth in Him sinneth not."[2] That is to say, no one is sinless, but he that abides in Christ does not abide in sin.

---

[1] Proverbs xx. 9.   [2] 1st Epistle of John i. 8 and iii. 6.

The unfilial feeling of the elder son shows itself in a half-unconscious way which is very remarkable, "Lo, these many years do I serve thee as a bondservant (δουλεύω),[1] and thou never gavest me (so much as) a kid, that I might make merry with my friends;" though the father's reply, "Son, thou art ever with me, and all that is mine is thine," shows that he was at liberty to invite whomsoever he pleased to his father's table. We may imagine his father answering in modern language, "You serve me these many years! No doubt—you are my heir, and in serving me you serve yourself. You never transgressed a commandment of mine! No doubt—and are my commandments grievous? I never gave you a kid whereon to feast with your friends! You have always been at liberty to invite them to my table; and if they do not like to dine with me, they are no fit companions for my son." But he gave the gentle and gracious answer, "Son, thou art ever with me, and all that is mine is thine," which, if the son had ears to hear, was a keener rebuke.

In the wish of the elder son that he could sometimes feast with his own friends, apart from his father, was contained the germ of that desire to escape the wholesome restraints of home, which, in its full development, had brought his brother first to riotous and wasteful living, and afterwards to the service of the stranger and the herding

---

[1] The remark as to the force of δουλεύω is made by Stier.

of swine. This root of sin is in us all, but in him it was not so full-grown as to bring forth death.[1] The purpose of this conversation is to show the special dangers of those who have never left the Father's house, and live all their lives in the habitual service of God; and, further, to show the safeguard against these dangers; namely, to appreciate the blessings of such a life as they deserve. The father's answer, "Son, thou art ever with me, and all that is mine is thine," was no new revelation; it might have been introduced with "remember"; he seemed to have forgotten it. We may imagine the father adding, "If thou hast not, it is because thou askest not."[2] What more could man or angel desire than this, to be a child of God, living from his birth in the light of his Father's presence, heir of his Father's treasures, and even now able to have whatever he wants for the asking? Nothing more is needed, except the spirit which appreciates these privileges and blessings. It was this spirit of thankful reception that was wanting to the elder son—he did not remember what his position was in his father's house. Had he rightly remembered it, he would not have wished to feast with his own friends apart from his father, and would have loved the Prodigal for the father's sake, if not for his own.

---

[1] James i. 15, Revised Version.
[2] "Ye have not, because ye ask not" (James iv. 2.) It is not at all unlikely that this may be a saying of Christ. This Epistle is full of allusions to Christ's recorded teaching.

There is an emphatic warning of the dangers of such a character in the message of Christ, in the Apocalypse, to the Ephesian Church—"I know thy works, and thy toil and thy patience; and thou hast patience, and hast borne for my name's sake, and hast not grown weary. But I have this against thee, that thou hast left thy first love. Remember therefore from whence thou art fallen, and repent, and do the first works; or else I come to thee, and will move thy candlestick out of its place, except thou repent."[1] This is exactly the state of the elder son's heart and life: true and sincere service of God, but without that love from the heart which He desires and demands. This "fall" of the Ephesian Church, we should observe, did not amount to apostasy. Christ allows a time for repentance. He does not say, "Thy candlestick is removed," or "Thy light is going out;" and it may be that the Ephesians, among whom, according to the accepted tradition, Saint John passed the last years of his life, heeded the warning, and repented, and returned to their first love. But though they had not lost their position, yet with their comparatively loveless service of Christ they were in danger of losing it. As the author of *Ecce Homo* truly says, "No virtue can be safe unless it is enthusiastic," though the enthusiasm has no need to be noisy or demonstrative. The elder son was such a one as those Ephesians. He was not an apostate; he was

---

[1] Rev. ii. 2, 5.

too prudent to think of leaving the father's house, and with it comfort, respectability, occupation which was probably agreeable, and his position as his father's heir. Such prudence is not to be despised; godliness is profitable both for the present life and that which is to come,[1] and there is a spiritual prudence which Our Lord constantly commends. But that which makes man likest God—unselfish love—was wanting; he was calculating towards his father, and unsympathising towards his brother.

We have now to consider the similar teaching of the parable of the Labourers in the Vineyard. The labourers who toiled in the vineyard from early morning are nearly the same as the elder son who had served his father all his life; and the murmurs of the labourers who had borne the burden of the day and the scorching heat, when those who had worked but one hour, and that in the evening, were paid as much as themselves, are nearly the same as the murmurs of the elder brother at seeing the returning prodigal received with rejoicing and festivity, and restored, without a word of reproach, to a son's place in the father's house and the father's love. And the answer to both is the same. God's service is unlike man's, in that mere length of service does not count in the apportioning of reward. When the repentance of the prodigal is sincere, he is at once restored to the place which his sins had forfeited; and when the service of the latest hired

---

[1] 1st Timothy iv. 8.

labourers is honest, they receive an equal reward with those who have toiled all day. "God giveth (and forgiveth) liberally, and upbraideth not."[1] We are accepted, not according to what we have done, but according to what we are.

Perhaps the impression which the majority of careless readers receive from this parable, is that it is possible to enter the service of God at any time of life, and at the end receive an equal reward with those who have served Him all their lives. This, however, is contradicted by the parable itself. To the question, "Why stand ye here all the day idle?" the answer was, "Because no man hath hired us." But if any of the labourers had in the middle of the day, or even early in the morning, refused the offer of work from mere idleness, and in reliance on the kindness of the owner of the vineyard, we cannot think they would have been permitted to come in at the eleventh hour; or if they had, they would not have received a day's wages for an hour's work. From the language and imagery of this parable alone it would be much more reasonable to infer that God's call to work in His vineyard, if once disregarded, will never be renewed. But no parable is meant to provide for all cases. The case of those who disregard God's call and their own privileges is not here touched on; but that of the Prodigal reveals a degree of longsuffering of God with sinners

---

[1] James i. 5. This also may be an unrecorded saying of Christ.

which man could not have dared to hope for; and in the parable of the Two Sons,[1] Our Lord tells of a son who at first refused to work in his father's vineyard, but afterwards changed his mind, and was permitted to go to work.

As for the acceptableness, or the possibility, of a "death-bed repentance," the parable of the Labourers in the Vineyard has no bearing on it whatever. Work cannot be begun on a death-bed; and to repent and be converted on a death-bed would be entering the vineyard, not at the eleventh but at the twelfth hour. It may be possible, but this parable alone gives no support for such a belief.

This parable, as we have seen, teaches that neither length of service nor quantity of work counts in the apportionment of the heavenly reward. But it is not true that all rewards are equal. Such a notion is contradicted by Our Lord in the conversation that led to this parable. Peter, contrasting himself and the rest of the twelve with the young ruler who had proved unable to give up all and follow Christ, inquired, "Lo, we have left all and followed Thee: what shall we have therefore?" To which the Lord replied, "Verily I say unto you, that ye which have followed me, in the regeneration (or restoration of all things—see Acts iii. 21), when the Son of Man shall sit on the throne of His glory, ye also shall sit on twelve thrones, judging (that is to say, ruling) the twelve tribes of Israel." We cannot tell

[1] Matt. xxi. 28.

the exact meaning of these mysterious words, but they evidently point to some high and peculiar honour which, in the eternal world, shall belong to those who in the present world have been foremost in the service of Christ; and if to the twelve, then also to Saint Paul, and to all others who have done and endured the most in His service. The same truth is clearly hinted in the parable of the Pounds,[1] where one servant of a nobleman who had been made a king is rewarded with the government of ten cities for the service of earning ten pounds for his master, and another servant with the government of five cities for the service of earning five pounds. But in the conversation now before us, having promised to His Apostles the highest reward which the imagination of an Israelite could conceive—to be viceroys over Israel in the Messiah's kingdom—the Lord changes His tone, and speaks the parable of the Labourers in the Vineyard, for the purpose of warning them that the expectation of such glory has its own temptations, and must not be too highly esteemed. In the same spirit, He said on another occasion, "In this rejoice not, that the spirits are subject unto you; but rejoice that your names are written in heaven."[2] And in a similar spirit, when speaking of the signs and wonders that were to be wrought in answer to the prayer of faith, He adds the warning, "When ye stand praying, forgive, if ye have ought against any one; that My Father which is in Heaven may

---

[1] Luke xix. 12. [2] Luke x. 20.

forgive you your trespasses." [1] In the passage before us He both introduces and concludes the parable of the Labourers in the Vineyard with the warning, "Many shall be last that are first, and first that are last;" showing that the highest rewards—including the Master's approval, which is the greatest of them all—do not necessarily belong to the longest service or to the greatest quantity of work done, or even to the most steadfast endurance of the "scorching heat" of persecution; but to those who show an unselfish, ungrudging, and unmurmuring spirit. The same words—"the last shall be first and the first last"—might have occurred at the end of the parable of the Prodigal: the elder son was first, but with his unloving Pharisaic spirit he was in danger of becoming last. It is the same teaching as that of Saint Paul, in a passage which is perhaps seldom thought of in connection with this parable: "Though I bestow all my goods to feed the poor, and though I give my body to be burned (a harder thing than to toil under the scorching noonday heat of summer in Palestine), and have not the charity that envieth not, seeketh not its own, is not easily provoked, and thinketh no evil, it profiteth me nothing." [2] But neither here, nor in the conversation between the father and the elder son, is there any threat of final and eternal condemnation, except the hint to the Pharisees implied in the words, "And the elder son was angry, and would not go in" (to the festival

[1] Mark xi. 25.   [2] 1 Cor. xiii. 3, 5.

with which his brother's return was welcomed); intimating that if they persisted in their exclusiveness, they would exclude themselves from the marriage feast of the King's Son.[1] It is true, as Our Lord, not long after, taught the disciples in the parable of the Ten Virgins,[2] that profession of Christ before the world, symbolised by the lamps, and legal purity of life, symbolised by virginity, will not avail to save without the true spirit of religion in the heart. But no one parable can teach all truth, or answer every question that may be raised upon it; and it is not in the least like the teaching of Christ, to hold that those who habitually serve God and keep all His commandments like the elder son, or live from youth to age in the unbroken service of God like the first hired labourers, are in danger of losing their eternal reward for a fit of anger or sullenness at a manifestation of Divine grace which they have not imagination enough to understand.[3]

In the warning at the end of the parable of the Labourers in the Vineyard, "Many that are first shall be last," there is no allusion to such a case as that of Judas, who, being one of the twelve, was among the first, and yet fell away altogether; for the crime by which Judas fell was not a deficiency in the love and charity taught by Christ, but a treason which

---

[1] Matt. xxii. 2.   [2] Matt. xxv. 1.

[3] The words at the end of the parable in the old text, "Many are called but few chosen," though elsewhere spoken by Our Lord, are now known to be spurious in this passage, and are rejected by the Revisers.

would have been judged worthy of death by an earthly tribunal. This warning has the same significance as His reply, when, on an earlier occasion, the disciples asked which of them was to be greatest in the kingdom of heaven; and the Lord answered, "Whosoever shall humble himself as this little child, the same is the greatest in the kingdom of heaven."[1] And when the two sons of Zebedee asked for the chief places in the kingdom, He told the disciples, "Whosoever would be first among you shall be (*i.e.* let him be) your servant."[2]

But in what sense is it true that length of service and quantity of work go for nothing in the Divine sight? Are patient trial and endurance to have no reward? are they to be, in the eternal world, as though they had never been? It cannot be so. It is true that

> Heaven rejects the lore
> Of nicely calculated less or more.[3]

But it is also true that "by works is faith made perfect"—"is made perfect," not only in the sense of "passes into action and becomes manifest," but in the deeper sense that when right works are done, not legally or mechanically but in a spirit of faith, they pass into character; and character is formed for eternity. For all, however, "boasting is excluded"; for "we are not under law but under grace."[4]

To sum up our conclusions. In each of these

---

[1] Matt. xviii. 1, 4.   [2] Matt. xx. 27.
[3] Wordsworth.   [4] Rom. iii. 27 and vi. 14.

parables there are two distinct lessons; one of them obvious, the other more recondite. In the parable of the Prodigal, the obvious lesson is that God forgives freely and without upbraiding, so that restoration is complete when repentance is sincere; that God welcomes repentant prodigals, and man ought to welcome them. In that of the Labourers, the obvious lesson is the kindred one, that those who enter the service of God late in life shall, if their service is sincere, be placed on an equality with those who have served God all their lives—that mere length of service and quantity of work do not count when the eternal recompenses are awarded. The more recondite lesson of the parable of the Prodigal is a warning against the special dangers of a life spent from the beginning in the service of God; the danger of such service becoming mechanical; the danger of trusting in one's own righteousness rather than in the grace of God, and of permitting an alienation of the heart from God to go on unchecked because unnoticed. And the more recondite lesson of the parable of the Labourers is the kindred one—that those who have done very lengthened or very eminent service to God are in danger of trusting in their own services, and of regarding with jealousy those who are placed on an equality with them after services which have been much shorter, or in the eyes of men much smaller. These two errors are the same in kind, and the proper safeguard against both is the same; namely, a truer appreciation of the privileges and blessings which are theirs as God's children, not on condition of works but of faith. The elder son is told by his father, "Thou art ever with me, and all that is mine is thine"; the first hired labourers go home to their eternal reward with the wages of a lifetime of toil and endurance in the master's service. No further blessing is needful or possible, except a right and thankful appreciation of that which they already enjoy.[1]

The elder son and the first hired labourers are typical men of the old moral world. Christ has taught us new and higher principles than theirs, but the Gospel must be based on the Law: Christ came not to destroy the Law but to fulfil it. Such men are certainly not typical Christians, but neither are the latest hired labourers, still less the returned prodigal: the typical Christian is the elder brother when he is reconciled to the returned prodigal;— the typical Christian is the labourer, who, after bearing the burden of the day and the scorching heat, learns graciously to acquiesce in his Master's action in placing on an equality with

---

[1] Stier quotes with approval Luther's saying that "they take their penny and are damned"; but this seems perversely wrong. The saying of the owner of the vineyard to the murmuring labourer, "Take that which is thine and go thy way," has nothing to do with "Depart, ye cursed," and means nothing harsher than "Cease this useless disputing, and go home to supper with thy well-earned wages"; for the imagery of the parable does not include any invitation to a dinner or supper, from which exclusion would be a punishment.

him the fellow-labourer who entered at the eleventh hour.

And underlying the double lesson of these two parables are the truths, not so much expressed as implied and taken for granted, that God is our Father, and seeks us because we are His children; that it is possible for man to spend his entire life, from the beginning, in the Father's house; and that to do so is the highest aim of Christian education and Christian life.[1]

[1] On the subject of such an education, see the late Dr. Horace Bushnell's *Christian Nurture* (Edinburgh, Strahan: London, Sampson Low, 1861), an excellent book which appears to be much less known than it deserves.

CHAPTER V.

NATURAL SELECTION IN THE SPIRITUAL WORLD.

It has been said, with some exaggeration, that Butler's entire work on the *Analogy of Religion to the Constitution of Nature* is a commentary on the text which he quotes from Origen, that "he who believes the Scripture to have proceeded from the Author of nature, may well expect to find the same sort of difficulties in it as are found in the constitution of nature."

Analogy is defined as resemblance of relations. When there are similar relations between similar things, analogical reasoning implies no principle more recondite than the legal maxim of "like case, like rule." But when the things between which the analogies subsist are unlike, the most difficult questions of philosophy may arise in determining whether the analogies are real; and, if they are real, what weight of inference they are able to bear. Now granting, what I regard as unquestionably true, that the books of Nature and of Revelation are two works by the same Divine Author, it appears to me not the less true that although they do present many and important real analogies—by the tracing of which Butler's great work has done imperishable service to religious philosophy—yet there is a fundamental unlikeness between Nature and Revelation, not in structure but in purpose, which totally excludes the analogy here indicated by Origen and by Butler.

If we know, or can conjecture, the purpose for which the world of Nature has been created—including in Nature the entire mortal life of man — this purpose is that it may be a nidus for the development of immortal life. This answer is not offered as a complete one; it seems probable that the universe of Nature serves many Divine purposes, whereof the greater number are undiscoverable by us.

> Lo, these are parts of His ways;
> And how small a whisper do we hear of Him!
> But the thunder of His power who can understand?[1]

This, however, is certain, that the world of Nature has not been created for our instruction. Living in the world, it is no doubt our duty and privilege to learn from it; but to say that this is the purpose for which it has been created, would be as complete an inversion of actual relations as to say that ships are built for the purpose of teaching the art of navigation. Now, of the Book of Revelation the opposite is true; that Book has been written for our instruction; and

[1] Job xxvi. 14.

it cannot reasonably be said that we ought to expect the same difficulties in the second as in the first. When an infinitely powerful and perfectly wise Being first uses His power in a way which we are able to understand only far enough to perceive His power and His wisdom, but with scarcely any insight into His purposes; and when He afterwards condescends to instruct those whose fate depends on His will; the principles of analogy do not lead to the expectation that His teaching will reproduce the difficulties of His unrevealed purposes and His unexplained action. Rather ought we to expect that His instruction will be instructive—that the Book which He has given us for our guidance will be found to clear up difficulties in that other work of His which has no such purpose. And I maintain that this is what we do find—that Revelation tends to clear up the difficulties of Nature. To say that Revelation *only* reproduces the difficulties of Nature, is as unsatisfactory a defence as if it were to be said that a translation is not more difficult than its original, or that a commentary introduces no difficulties which were not in the text.

I have made these remarks in order to introduce the consideration of a real analogy between the natural and the spiritual worlds, whereof the existence is pointed out in one of the best-known passages of Butler's great work, though its true significance has been revealed only by the progress of science in our own time. I refer to the passage where he speaks of the waste of seeds, as follows :—[1]

"The viciousness of the world is, in different ways, the great trial[2] which renders it a state of virtuous discipline to good men. That which appears amidst the general corruption is, that there are some persons who, having within them the principles of amendment and recovery, attend to and follow the notices of virtue and religion which are afforded them; and that the present world is not only an exercise of virtue in these persons, but an exercise of it in ways and degrees peculiarly apt to improve it, even beyond what would be by the exercise of it required in a perfectly virtuous society. But that the present world does not actually become a state of moral discipline to the generality—that they do not improve or grow better in it—cannot be urged as a proof that it was not intended for moral discipline, by any who at all observe the analogy of nature. For of the numerous seeds of vegetables which are adapted to improve to maturity and perfection, we do not see perhaps that one in a million actually does. Yet no one will deny that those seeds which do attain to that maturity and perfection answer the end for which they were designed by nature. And I cannot forbear adding, though it is not to the present purpose, that the appearance of such an amazing waste

---

[1] *Analogy*, Fitzgerald's edition, p. 104.
[2] I have substituted *trial* for *temptation*, which latter word has ceased to be used in this sense.

in nature with respect to those seeds by foreign causes is to us as unaccountable as, what is much more terrible, the present and future ruin of so many moral agents by themselves."[1]

This passage—at least its last sentence—has been called a "cruel platitude"; but most unjustly. Butler had not the slightest taint of cruelty in his nature; his sense of human sinfulness was almost morbidly acute, but he had nothing whatever of that fierce delight in the thought of the Divine vengeance upon it which has animated such men as Tertullian and Jonathan Edwards. He was a logician, and, though I believe he fell into errors in the application of the principles of analogy, he was aware that no analogy is perfect; he could not fail to perceive that this analogy fails in those particulars which are in themselves the most important — namely, that seeds, unlike "moral agents," have neither power to sin nor capacity to suffer; but he thought it needless to remind his readers of anything so obvious. I admit, however, that this remark of Butler's may naturally, though not quite reasonably, excite indignation at a first reading; and he was deficient in the great literary virtue of sympathy with the reader. But to return to the consideration of the entire

[1] This passage was probably suggested by 2nd Esdras viii. 41 :—"For as the husbandman soweth much seed upon the ground, and planteth many trees, and yet the thing that is sown good in its season cometh not up, neither doth all that is planted take root; even so is it of them that are sown in the world—they shall not all be saved."

passage quoted. It is not a platitude; on the contrary, it is an acute and sagacious set of observations, by no means obvious, and yet perfectly true except in the concluding sentence, which treats of a subject —namely, the apparent waste of seeds—whereof the true bearing was not, and could not be, understood at any time before the publication of Darwin's great work on the Origin of Species.

The full title of that work is *The Origin of Species by means of Natural Selection, or the preservation of Favoured Races in the Struggle for Life.* As the word Darwinism, in common language, is often used as a mere synonym for the entire doctrine of organic Evolution, and as the fundamental conceptions of Darwin's theory, though certainly true, are by no means obvious, I shall give an account, in outline, first of the general doctrine of Evolution, and then of Darwin's attempt to explain organic Evolution by means of Natural Selection.

The theory of Evolution, stated in the most general terms, is merely this, that everything has become what it is by a gradual process under natural law. In the organic world, Evolution means that not only every individual organism has been evolved out of a simple germ by a process of ever-increasing complication, but that species and classes have been produced by descent, with modification, from other and simpler species and classes; so that it is possible, and perhaps probable, though for want of evidence not demonstrable, that all the individuals of every species and every class in both the vegetable and the animal kingdoms, are the descendants of a single organism, having a structure as simple as that of the first germs of the existing organisms; into which life, with all its powers and capacities, was in the beginning breathed by the Creator.

Supposing the fact of organic Evolution to be proved, and I believe that it is amply proved, not by demonstrative but by cumulative evidence; the question next arises, by what agency it is effected: and Darwin's theory is an attempt to answer this. Supposing his theory to be true, which, on the whole, I do not grant, it is related to the general doctrine of Evolution as the explanation is related to the facts to be explained; as, for instance, Newton's theory of gravitation to Kepler's laws of the celestial motions:—Kepler showed what in fact the motions are; Newton showed how they are the necessary result of simple fundamental laws.

The fundamental laws, or facts, whereon Darwin has based his theory, are simple and familiar. With all organisms, animal and vegetable alike, the rate of increase by reproduction is very high, so that, if all germs attained to maturity, there would not be room for all, or nearly all, to live; and hence is a necessity for the premature destruction, mentioned in the passage quoted above from Butler, of the vast majority of the seeds of plants, and the eggs and young of animals.

Another fundamental fact is that, although all

organisms propagate after their kind and likeness, yet the resemblance of offspring to parent is not rigidly close, but admits of slight variations. The conditions and causes of these variations of the offspring from the parent form constitute a most obscure physiological question; but it appears certain that such variation is promoted by slight changes in the conditions of life.

Darwin's entire theory is based on these two obvious facts: the high rate of natural increase throughout the entire organic creation, necessitating the destruction of the greater part of the germs which are produced; and the tendency of the offspring to differ, however slightly, from the parent form. The high rate of increase, leading to the destruction of the vast majority of germs, causes a "struggle for life"; and this prevails in vegetable species as much as in animal ones: thickly-sown seedlings, whereof the weaker perish because they are deprived of sunshine by the stronger, are engaged in the struggle for life, no less than animals which fight with each other for food. And from the fact of variability, it follows that some individuals must have points of superiority—strength to obtain food, or fleetness to escape enemies, or any of the innumerable points which may give to one some advantage over another; those which have any such advantage will, on the average and on the whole, be the most likely to succeed and to survive, and to leave offspring; which, on the average and on the whole, will inherit their superiorities; and this process will go on, accumulating through successive generations.

Thus the high rate of natural increase causes a struggle for life; variation produces favoured races, and the automatic action of natural selection, giving the race to the swift and the battle to the strong, ensures the "survival of the fittest" by preserving the favoured races, which are the best worth preserving, while destroying the rest.

It has been said that this does not explain the origin of species at all, but only their preservation after they have been originated. I agree, on the whole, with this criticism.[1]

It remains, however, true that natural selection among spontaneous variations must tend to improvement; and it is also true that it must tend to what Darwin calls Divergence of Character; the improvement is effected on divergent lines. This necessarily occurs as a result of the struggle for life in a world where different ways of life are open, and where individuals and races may be benefited in different ways by different kinds of superiority. To mention an obvious instance; if, among a species of wild dogs,

---

[1] A great part of my work on *Habit and Intelligence* is occupied with an attempt, which cannot be here stated in even the slightest summary, to prove that organic Evolution cannot be accounted for by any Darwinian process of fortuitous variation and automatic natural selection; and that the theory of organic Evolution not only admits of, but demands, a Guiding Intelligence.

some individuals, or some families—for the members of the same family are likely to present the same variation—if some families vary from the parent stock in the direction of greater speed, others in the direction of greater strength, and others again in the direction of acuter scent; these, gaining their food in different ways, will tend to adopt different modes of life, and probably to inhabit different parts of the country. Thus natural selection will act on divergent lines. Distinct races will be formed, having different characters; and the separation of their lives will prevent them from mingling, and keep them distinct.

It is certain that the Darwinian process must be actually operative; it is certain that spontaneous variations must occur, and that the fittest must in general be preserved by natural selection in the struggle for life. For our present purpose it is needless to discuss the degree of importance which is to be assigned to this agency. Among believers in Evolution—and all naturalists are now probably believers in it—opinions on the importance of the Darwinian process as a factor of Evolution vary from that of Weissmann, who thinks it has been the sole and exclusive cause, to that of Mr. Seebohm, the eminent ornithologist, who thinks its only effect on the process of Evolution has been to increase its rapidity;[1] but none doubts that it has been an actual factor in the evolutionary process.

Now, this is sufficient for clearing up the difficulty

[1] See note at end of chapter.

respecting the waste of seeds whereon Butler insists in the passage quoted above. For, without the high rate of increase, and the consequent great destruction of seeds and germs, there would be no struggle for life; without the struggle for life there would be no natural selection; and without natural selection to weed out the unfit and to preserve the fit, there would be perhaps no improvement whatever, and certainly much less and much slower improvement than that which actually has been. Thus what appeared, and could not but appear, to Bishop Butler as an apparent failure of Creative purpose, is now seen to be a necessary part of the Creative plan. All special difficulty from the waste of seeds disappears. And, though it is a mystery why pain should be permitted at all among animals, which have no moral nature which can either deserve it as vengeance ($\tau\iota\mu\omega\rho\acute{\iota}\alpha$), or derive benefit from it as correction ($\kappa\acute{o}\lambda\alpha\sigma\iota\varsigma$), yet the perplexity is lightened when we understand that the conflict which is the cause of suffering to individuals, tends nevertheless to the advancement of the race. Unimproved and inferior races are superseded, crushed out, and destroyed, but room is thus made for the improved and superior races. Evil is made to work for ultimate good; the good prevails, survives, and remains, while the evil is destroyed. All evil is self-destructive, and is doomed to extinction.

Another principle is at the same time shown to prevail in the working of nature; namely, that all improvement has its rise from isolated beginnings. When it is the purpose of the Creator to produce a new and improved race out of an old one, the end is not attained by simultaneously improving the entire parent race : on the contrary, the Creator's method is to improve, by the inscrutable process which we call spontaneous variation, a few individuals or families of the old race; these prevail and multiply, and give origin to a new and improved race, which, it may be, supersedes the old.

Another general principle is here shown; namely, that equality is no part of the Creator's purpose. This is little more than another statement of the truth that entire races are not improved in mass, but improvement begins at particular points. It would appear, moreover, that the Creator's purpose is not improvement simply, but improvement on as many divergent lines as possible. This is shown, not merely by the "divergence of character" under the Darwinian law whereof we have already spoken, but (as I have elsewhere endeavoured to prove) by many facts of morphology and classification, which the exclusively Darwinian theory scarcely attempts to explain.[1]

So far as we can trace the Divine purpose in Creation, that purpose appears to be the production of the highest and the most varied excellence; this excellence is in great part attained by conflict; and it is no part of that purpose either to let all

[1] See *Habit and Intelligence*, 2nd edition, chapters xiii. xiv. and xviii.

start equally in the conflict, or to bring all to an equality when it is ended. On the contrary, Creative purpose aims not at the highest average of excellence, but at the highest degree and the greatest variety of excellence.

The same laws and agencies of progress which we have seen to prevail in the world of organic life, prevail also in political, moral and spiritual life—not merely analogous laws and agencies, but the same. It is one of the most familiar truths, that in human society all improvement begins from individuals; a new truth never dawns at first on a multitude; when it has made itself known to a few, it has still to struggle for general reception; and in the world of human thought and action, as in the world of organic life, progress is due to free competition and the victory and preservation of the best. It is only in virtue of this principle that freedom can be justified. The ever-repeated argument against freedom is that when the mass of mankind have attained it, they do not know how to use it aright; and this may be true; but freedom is none the less right and good. As, in the organic world, very many more seeds are produced than can be matured, so, in the human world, an immensely large proportion of effort is, and must be, wasted. But it is only by permitting freedom of effort in all directions, with its unavoidable concomitant of waste, that any valuable results can be achieved. Open careers may tempt men to waste their lives in positions for which they are unfit, yet careers must be open in order that, on the whole, the best men may be selected. Commercial freedom may tempt men into disastrous enterprises, but commerce and industry must be free in order to learn, by actual trial and competition, how the industry of men and nations may be most profitably directed. Freedom of thought, speech, and publication, may lead to the dissemination of pernicious error, yet such freedom is necessary to the progress of thought and knowledge, and free and fair discussion is the only means whereby error can be defeated and destroyed. In a word, it is necessary that in human society there shall be full freedom, within the limits of public safety, for the spontaneous variation of action and thought, in order that the best results may be selected and preserved by competition, while the worthless ones perish.[1]

The truths which are the most conspicuously shown in the conflict both of the organic world and the world of human life and effort, are these two: that improvement begins from individual centres, and that progress is achieved through conflict. The same principles hold in what is properly the spiritual world—in the secret recesses of character,

> The abysmal deeps of personality,[2]

---

[1] This paragraph is taken, with a little alteration and condensation, from *Habit and Intelligence*, 2nd edition, pp. 565, 566.

[2] Tennyson's *Palace of Art*.

where man meets God alone. And what is most prominent in the purely spiritual domain, is a further development of the truth that progress begins from individuals. It is best expressed in the words of the greatest moral Teacher whom the world has ever seen or ever can see: "Whosoever hath, to him shall be given, and he shall have abundance; but whosoever hath not, from him shall be taken away even that which he hath."[1] This is expressed in the language of our theory by saying that moral and spiritual improvement tend to continue on the same lines whereon they have begun. This saying was a favourite one with Our Lord. He once repeated it with the variation, "Whosoever hath not, from him shall be taken away even that which he thinketh he hath (or, seemeth to have)."[2]

Thus we learn from the organic world and the world of human society, that progress does not begin with any action either by the mass, or directly upon the mass, but with individuals; and we find that in the spiritual world this tendency is not counteracted but strengthened.

Such are the facts and laws of nature. But man appears to have much difficulty in reconciling himself to them. Most nations, in most periods of their history, have been busy in constructing or maintaining barriers of restriction, "protection," and privilege, against the healthful and beneficent action of competition and freedom. And there appears to

[1] Matt. xiii. 12.   [2] Luke viii. 18, Revised Version.

be a general and deeply-seated feeling, that the highest justice demands equality. In Our Lord's parable of the Pounds,[1] when the servant who had done nothing for his master with the pound which had been entrusted to him, was condemned in the words, "Take away from him the pound, and give it unto him that hath the ten pounds," those that heard it remonstrated, saying, "Lord, he hath ten pounds." It does not matter whether we understand this as said by the fellow-servants in the parable, or by the hearers of the parable; in either case, it represents current opinion; and Christ, in reply, contradicted it by repeating the maxim, "Unto every one that hath shall be given; but from him that hath not, even that which he hath shall be taken away from him." Yet this, in the case of the "unprofitable servant" who had made no use of the pound committed to his charge, was the most evident justice; and the stern saying that "From him who hath not, shall be taken away even that which he hath" may, in its application to the moral and spiritual world, be thus paraphrased, "From him who has neglected or misused the means of good offered to him, the means themselves shall be taken away."[2] And the other form of the saying, "From him who hath not, shall be taken away even

---

[1] Luke xix. 12, 26.

[2] See the Rev. Henry Latham's *Pastor Pastorum, or the Schooling of the Apostles by Our Lord* (Deighton, Bell, and Co., 1890), pp. 312, 316. I hope this work is attaining the position which it deserves, as a classic of Biblical study.

that which he thinketh that he hath," may likewise be paraphrased, "The time shall come when all disguises and all self-deception shall be stripped away, and he who has nothing shall see himself as he is."[1]

"The aphorism that to him that hath, more is given, was, as applied to material wealth, in some form or other probably familiar to the shrewd men of the time. But what was startling was, that this principle should be adopted by Christ, and laid down as one of those upon which God's government is carried on. For this inequality in human conditions, and the tendency to rise faster the higher one gets, and to sink faster the lower one falls, was a thing that was commonly regarded as a defect in the world's arrangement, due to some inherent perversity in matter or in man. People's minds in those days were possessed with the notion that God must have intended to make things fair and equal for all, but that inequalities had slipped into the world in the making; soon, however, the Messiah would come and set this right among other things. Hence it startled Our Lord's hearers to find this defect, as they deemed it, in the order of the world brought forward by Him, and not only not explained away as they would have expected, but set forth among the laws according to which the spiritual order of the world was carried on."

"Our Lord, as a fact, asserts not only that

[1] Compare Rev. iii. 17.

inequalities widen, but also that they are purposely so widened. Spiritual progress was to be brought about after the plan upon which all other human progress proceeds. It was to originate in individuals, who should push forward, seize upon posts in the foreground, and hold them till the rest came up. It is not the way of humanity to advance in line along the whole front; all progress comes of individual excellence, and the world is so ordered as to favour the growth of one beginning to out-top the rest."[1]

All experience confirms the truth of this: of its apparent ungraciousness, or unsuitability to a Gospel of grace, we shall have to speak in the following chapter. But it is not only as certain a fact as any fact of observation can be: it is also an obviously necessary result of the constitution of things. "There is need of strong men for human progress. If life were smooth and easy, men would as it were advance in line, and the stronger men would not so surely come in front of the rest. It is in times of trouble that men are most apt to recognise worth and capacity, and make much of them. So that the trials and difficulties of human life which come of evil, have this good effect among others, that they help to pick out the men who are fitted to be the leaders of human movements and of human thought."[2] And this, though originally a law of mere nature, was purposely adopted by Christ as part of His

[1] *Pastor Pastorum*, pp. 313, 315.   [2] *Ibid.* p. 45.

method of teaching and government. It was to those of the Apostles who had learned the most of His mind and spirit, that He accorded the marvellous privilege of witnessing His heavenly glory on the Mount of Transfiguration.[1]

This principle, that to those who have shall be given, is not, so far as I am aware, brought into prominence in the Old Testament : but the preceding principle, of which it is a development, that progress begins with individuals and not with multitudes,—this has been the Divine method from the first. The first step taken in history towards the Divine aim of the formation of a Church which was ultimately to include all mankind, was the calling of Abraham to be the father of a chosen people, through whom Prophecy and Revelation were to be given to man, and of whose race according to the flesh the Son of God was to be born, to the end that in Him all the kindreds of the earth should be blessed. And all the history of the Chosen People shows that among them—as in every history that has to relate anything worth achieving—the Providential method of progress is to raise up chosen men, teachers, and leaders, from time to time: Moses, David, Isaiah, and all the long line of heroes, prophets, saints, and martyrs, leading up to Him who is eminently the chosen of God, even Christ.

To sum up our results :—It is an obvious fact that

[1] *Pastor Pastorum*, p. 143.

the world is ordered on a basis of inequality; in the organic world, as Darwin has shown, it is of inequality —of favoured races—that all progress comes; and we have seen that history shows the same to be true of the human and spiritual world. All human progress is due to elect human individuals; elect not only to be a blessing to themselves, but still more to be a blessing to multitudes of others. Any superiority, whether in the natural or in the mental and spiritual world, becomes a vantage-ground for gaining a greater superiority. Of the origin of these superiorities we know but little; in the language of science they are ascribed to accidental spontaneous variation— a phrase which candidly confesses our ignorance—but in the language of faith they are ascribed to the guidance of Divine Providence. It is the method of the Divine government, acting in the provinces both of Nature and of Grace, that all benefit should come to the many through the elect few.

"So here," some reader will perhaps exclaim, "we have the discarded doctrine of election brought back in a scientific disguise!"

No, not the theological dogma of election. The so-called doctrine is a fact of nature—not a revealed truth, but an observed fact—and true of the natural world, irrespectively of the spiritual world. But all who, even in the vaguest way, accept the prophetic character of the history which began with Abraham and led up to Christ, must perceive that the Divine method of progress in that history was to influence the mass through elect individuals. And Christ afterwards said to the spiritual children of Abraham, "Ye are the salt of the earth; ye are the light of the world"[1]—the salt which preserves a sinful world from total corruption, and the light of a world which but for them would have lain in darkness. Nature, history, reason, and revelation, unite in teaching that the Divine way of doing good and furthering progress is through "favoured races" and elect Churches; and the progress is due to the victory and survival of the best, who are naturally selected; the selection is natural, that is to say, it is wrought in the natural course of things. This constitutes an analogy between the Divine methods in the Kingdoms of Nature and of Grace, both closer and more important than any of those insisted on by Professor Drummond in his *Natural Law in the Spiritual World*.

It appears in the highest degree probable that the same is true in the spiritual and eternal world. We are not taught to regard that world as one of mere restful happiness; on the contrary, Christ's parable of the Pounds describes it as a world of effort and active service.[2] All who believe in the existence of an eternal world, where the spiritual elements of our present life shall be continued in existence free from the entangling restraint of its material elements and surroundings, believe also that the good will there be victorious and the evil defeated; and it is scarcely

---

[1] Matt. v. 13, 14.
[2] "Have thou authority over ten cities," Luke xix. 17.

possible to doubt that this will be effected as part of the natural order and course of things, and will thus be a case of progress by the natural selection of the fittest. For, by the nature of things, virtue tends to prevail; and when this is defeated, it is due either to the want of time for that tendency to work out its natural results, or to the counteraction of influences which belong to the material and not to the moral world, and are, in the logical sense, merely accidental to the latter. But in the eternal world there will be unlimited time for such tendencies to work out their natural and legitimate results; and it cannot be doubted that all counteracting agencies shall be removed.[1]

[1] The foregoing paragraph contains, in an extremely condensed form and in modern language, some of the most important ideas and arguments of the third chapter of the first part of Butler's *Analogy of Religion*.

NOTE TO CHAPTER V.

The following extract is from Mr. Seebohm's work on *The Geographical Distribution of the Charadriidae*, or the Plovers, Sandpipers, Snipes, and their allies :—

"But when we admit that the exhaustive arguments in favour of the theory of Evolution, propounded by Darwin in his remarkable work on the Origin of Species, prove its truth, so far as speculations on such remote events are capable of proof, we may at the same time doubt whether natural selection can be in any sense the cause of the origin of species. It has probably played a very important part in the history of evolution; its *rôle* has been that of increasing the rapidity with which the process of development has proceeded. Of itself it has probably been absolutely powerless to originate a species; the machinery by which species have been evolved has been completely independent of natural selection, and could have produced all the results which we call the evolution of species without its aid; though the process would have been slow had there been no struggle for life to increase its pace."

CHAPTER VI.

THE FINAL DESTINY OF THE REJECTED.

In the organic world, the rejection of the unfit is final; those living beings which are overpowered in the struggle for life perish, never to rise again. Is it the same in the spiritual world? Is there a resurrection for the elect only, or for all? and if the rejected of the present dispensation are raised up to a future existence, is it that they may be made fit for the Kingdom of God, or only that they may suffer the punishment of the sins which they committed on earth?

In reply to this last question, if we believe in a future life at all we cannot doubt the reality of retribution. In other words, the law of cause and effect, under which actions pass into character and character passes into destiny, is continued into the future life for both good and evil. "He that soweth to his flesh shall of the flesh reap corruption, and he that soweth to the Spirit shall of the Spirit reap eternal life."[1] "He that soweth sparingly shall reap

[1] Gal. vi. 8.

also sparingly, and he that soweth bountifully shall reap also bountifully." [1]

But it does not follow that the Divine anger which is to be reaped by sinners will be continued without end and without hope. The experience of nature is that

> All suffering doth destroy, or is destroyed; [2]

and the horrible thought of vengeance which has no purpose beyond itself, and of suffering which tends neither to heal the sin nor to end the existence of the sinner, is contrary to all the analogy of nature. So far as our experience reaches, all pain tends to destroy life, and consequently to bring about its own extinction.

But is there hope in a future life for the rejected of the present dispensation? On this question nature speaks with an uncertain voice. The most obvious inference from the analogy of nature is that they share the fate of wasted seeds; but obvious analogies may be only superficial. We have seen that in mental and spiritual as well as in merely organic life, improvement begins from elect races and individuals. But the analogy is incomplete; the improvement is propagated in a totally different way in the two cases. In organic life it is by natural descent; and even if it were otherwise possible, any improvement of the rejected races is excluded by the fact that their destruction is needed in order to make

---

[1] 2 Cor. ix. 6. [2] Byron.

room for the multiplication of the elect and naturally-selected races. In the moral and spiritual world, on the contrary, improvement is propagated not by natural descent but by spiritual influence; and in the Kingdom of God there will be no want of room for all to develop.

It is certain that the present Providential government of both the natural and the spiritual worlds has for its purpose the perfecting of the elect. But in the organic world, the rejection and destruction of the unfit is only the other side of a benevolent selection; and this real, though veiled, benevolence of the Creative purpose in nature, suggests that the Creator will hereafter allow them opportunity to realise those possibilities which in this life they failed to attain; or if this is impossible for any reason unknown to us, that they may at least be permitted to pass out of existence.

Further; the Darwinian principle of progress in the organic world by strife and competition, is not a moral principle — not contrary to morality, but beneath it. In human history, no doubt, strife and competition become agencies of moral advancement, by reason of the tendency of such qualities as fidelity and self-devotion to give the victory. But the highest virtues cannot enter into competition; competition is not a moral agency but destructive of morality, when it enters into a higher region than that to which it rightly belongs—into the relation between husband and wife, and between parents and children; in a word, into the family, which is the nearest approach to the Kingdom of God that the world of nature contains. And the higher is the moral standard which man sets before himself, the less does society yield to the right of the strong, and the more does it recognise the claims of the weak. The Darwinian principle, if it were applied in what is properly the moral domain, would condemn the weak, the infirm, and the destitute to perish in the conflict of life; but the highest human morality, on the contrary, which is that of Him who will not break a bruised reed, nor quench the dimly-burning wick of a lamp,[1] has learned to give them protection, and endeavours to secure what enjoyment of life is possible to them. It is important to note that this morality—this conscience—which protects those who cannot protect themselves, being anti-Darwinian, cannot have been evolved by any Darwinian process.[2] All this is at least a forcible suggestion that election, and the preservation of favoured races and individuals, are not the last words, nor the ultimate facts, of the Providential government of the universe.

Moreover, although the method of conferring blessing on the many through the elect few is continued under the present dispensation, yet the first step has been already taken towards superseding it by a law of equality. The distinction of races—of Jew and

---

[1] Isaiah xlii. 3.
[2] See R. H. Hutton's *Theological Essays*, p. 63. Strahan, 1871.

Gentile — has been abolished; "the Gentiles are fellow-heirs" of the blessings of the race of Abraham. Abraham and his family were called apart from the rest of the nations in order to qualify them for becoming a blessing to all nations; but it is evident that this separation could be no more than temporary and provisional; when the blessing was matured and complete, it was time for the separation to end. In Christ there is no distinction between the Jew and the Gentile, none between the Greek and the barbarian; not even between the Greek and the Scythian, the most barbarous of all barbarians;[1] or, to use corresponding modern language, no distinction between the European and the African. And the institution of hereditary priesthood, which was so deeply rooted in the religions of antiquity, and was adopted into Judaism, has found no place in Christianity; there is not, I believe, any church whatever calling itself by the name of Christ, in which the ministry is hereditary.

We have now to consider the teaching of Revelation on the subject of hope for the rejected of the present dispensation; but before we examine particular passages, there are some general remarks to be made. First, as to principles of interpretation. The most obvious interpretation is not necessarily the true

---

[1] Col. iii. 11. Although $\beta\acute{a}\rho\beta a\rho o s$ has not exactly the same connotations as our word "barbarian," it is obvious that Saint Paul has here such a climax in his thought.

one. The most obvious interpretation of the Messianic prophecies of the Old Testament, for instance, was that the Messiah should reign in warlike might and glory or in peaceful splendour;[1] it was by no means obvious, until the prophecies were fulfilled, that He would at first appear, not in the royal majesty foretold by David, but in the guise of the suffering Servant of God foretold by Isaiah;[2] if texts ought to be merely counted and not weighed, the Jews were right to whom a crucified Christ was a stumbling-block and an offence.[3] So it is with the doctrine of a final restoration. If we are merely to count texts, the doctrine of Holy Scripture is that the future state is hopeless for the rejected of the present dispensation; that in them shall be fulfilled the prayer of the Psalmist, "Let the sinners be consumed out of the earth, and let the wicked be no more;"[4] that their end shall be destruction of soul and body in Gehenna;[5] not, indeed, endless existence in a state of punishment, but final and hopeless destruction by the vengeance of God.[6] But if we weigh texts instead of merely counting them—if we look below the surface, and endeavour to read their inner meaning—

---

[1] See Psalms ii. lxxii. and cx.   [2] Isaiah l. and liii.
[3] See *The Larger Hope*, a sequel to *Salvator Mundi*, by Samuel Cox, D.D.
[4] Psalm civ. 35.   [5] Matt. x. 28.
[6] See Edward White's *Life in Christ*, which shows that the great majority of the passages of Scripture where future judgment is denounced, appear to teach that God's vengeance on sinners will be finally and utterly destructive.

God will give that which was a valley of troubling for a door of hope.[1]

God is angry with sin; this is Law. God desires to heal sin; this is Gospel. It is a true instinct in man which expects the attributes of Justice and of Mercy to be combined in a perfectly righteous Judge. But though these are co-eternal in the mind of God, yet it was necessary that, in the order of historical evolution, Law should be manifested first. It is the method of Our Lord, and of the Prophets and Apostles generally, to state apparently opposing truths, and to let their reconciliation take care of itself. But how God can be at once perfectly just and perfectly merciful; how retribution and forgiveness can both be parts of His purpose; how the elect of the present dispensation are comparatively few, but are elected that they may be the channel of ultimate blessing to all; these truths do not appear difficult to reconcile, when we remember the further truth that God has endless ages in which to work out His gracious purposes. The high and lofty One, whose Name is Holy, inhabiteth eternity.[2]

No doubt it is easy to quote a catena of passages of Holy Scripture which appear to assert that the Divine vengeance on sin is final and irreversible. But it is equally easy to quote a catena of passages which appear to assert that sin cannot be forgiven at all. "The soul that sinneth, it shall die."[3] "He that doeth wrong shall receive for the wrong that he

---

[1] Hosea ii. 15.   [2] Isaiah lvii. 15.   [3] Ezek. xviii. 4.

hath done, and there is no respect of persons."[1] Yet all who call themselves Christians "believe in the forgiveness of sins."

Next, as to the relation of the elect to the rejected. God's elect do not always value and use their blessings aright. Sometimes they value their privileges, not indeed too highly, but in a selfish and exclusive spirit, like the elder brother who was angry when the returned prodigal was restored to the place in the father's house which he had abandoned and forfeited. They are often, to their own great and grievous loss, slow to receive things outside their own election; they often fail to see that they are elect, not only to receive a blessing for themselves, but to be a channel of blessing to the rest; so that "the election of some, and the final salvation of all, may both be seen as consistent parts of one purpose."[2] Israel was the elect of the former dispensation, yet the calling of the Gentiles was a stumbling-block to the Israelites of the Apostolic age; and in the present age many of God's elect—elect not only to Christian privileges, but, I have no doubt, to a place in Christ's eternal Kingdom—denounce as heresy the doctrine of a general restoration; being, as yet, unable to see that the purpose of their election, as of that of the Israel of old, is not only to show the grace of God towards themselves, but to make them, ultimately, channels of grace to the rejected of the present

[1] Col. iii. 25.
[2] Jukes's *Names of God in Holy Scripture*, p. 105.

dispensation. How this is to be we know not; but Christ teaches us in His parable of the Pounds, that faithful service in the present life shall be rewarded with opportunities of greater service hereafter;[1] and no service can be higher than that of helping to save the lost. To those who call it heresy confidently to cherish these hopes, we, who believe in the ultimate universal victory of good, may reply in the words of Saint Paul: "After the way which they call heresy, so serve we the God of our (spiritual) fathers, believing all things which are according to the law, and which are written in the prophets; having hope towards God, which these also themselves look for, that there shall be a resurrection of the dead, both of the just and unjust."[2] For, believing that the sinner shall be saved through the condemnation of his sin, we look with hope for the resurrection of the unjust as well as of the just.

We shall now make a closer examination of the teaching of Holy Scripture on this subject. The prophecies of the Old Testament are full of promises of the ultimate restoration of Israel after all his sins; and they predict that the blessing of the last days shall not be poured forth on Israel alone, but on all nations, even those which have wandered the farthest from God.

One of the most remarkable of these is contained in the 16th chapter of Ezekiel. The entire chapter

---

[1] Luke xix. 12 et s [2] Acts xxiv. 14, 15.

is addressed to Jerusalem, and the greater part of it is filled with denunciations of her unfaithfulness, ingratitude, and sin; she is declared to be more hateful than the heathen Sodom or the apostate Samaria. But at the end the Spirit of Prophecy relents, and the Prophet writes:

"I will turn again their captivity, the captivity of Sodom and her daughters, and the captivity of Samaria and her daughters, and the captivity of thy captives in the midst of them. . . . And thy sisters, Sodom and her daughters, shall return to their former estate, and Samaria and her daughters shall return to their former estate, and thou and thy daughters shall return to your former estate." [1]

It is evident that in the case of Sodom, at least, the restoration cannot be national, because Sodom and its people had ceased to exist more than a thousand years before Ezekiel wrote. The promised restoration can only be spiritual, and in the eternal world. I do not say that so far-reaching a doctrine as that of final restoration could be safely rested on a single passage like this, which is no doubt in some degree symbolical; but it is very important as a parallel, from the Old Testament, to Saint Paul's prophecy of the ultimate salvation of the Gentiles,[2] whereof we shall speak farther on. It is also to be observed that the Apostle Jude mentions the case of Sodom as typical: "Even as Sodom and Gomorrah and the cities about them . . . are set forth *for an*

---

[1] Ezek. xvi. 53, 55.   [2] Rom. xi. 25 *et seq.*

example (δεῖγμα), suffering the vengeance (δίκην) of eternal fire."[1]

Moreover, although the prophecy now quoted from Ezekiel is probably the most remarkable special prophecy of restoration in any part of the Old Testament, excepting "the great prophecy of Israel's restoration" in the second part of Isaiah, yet it does not by any means stand alone. The 48th and 49th chapters of Jeremiah consist of denunciations of wrath against Moab and Ammon; but they thus end: "Yet will I bring again the captivity of Moab in the latter days, saith the Lord." "But afterward will I bring again the captivity of the children of Ammon, saith the Lord." As in the case of Sodom, these prophecies admit of only a spiritual fulfilment, because Moab and Ammon have long ceased to exist as nations.

In like manner the 19th chapter of Isaiah is entitled "The burden of Egypt," and is chiefly filled with denunciations of wrath; but at the end comes a promise of the return of the Egyptians to the true worship of God; and the Prophet goes on: "And the Lord shall smite Egypt, smiting and healing; and they shall return unto the Lord, and He shall be entreated of them, and shall heal them." In conclusion, Egypt, and that other great embodiment of godless might, Assyria, are set on an equality with the chosen people of God: "In that day shall Israel be the third with Egypt and with Assyria, a blessing in the midst of the earth; for that the Lord of

[1] Jude 7.

Hosts hath blessed them, saying, Blessed be Egypt my people, and Assyria the work of my hands, and Israel mine inheritance."[1] *The Lord shall smite, smiting and healing.* Observe, this is not said of Israel but of Egypt; we are here taught that all God's judgments are for ultimate mercy. And in the only psalm ascribed to Moses, we are taught that destruction is for ultimate restoration. "Thou turnest man to destruction, and sayest, Return, ye children of men."[2]

The threatenings and the promises of the Old Testament are mostly addressed to nations. But the first promise of restoration that we meet with, and perhaps the most emphatic in the Old Testament, is for mankind; and it admits of none but a purely spiritual interpretation. I mean the sentence of Jehovah on the Serpent. In the moment of his triumph at the loss of Paradise by Man, the Lord says to him: "I will put enmity between thee and the woman, and between thy seed and her seed; it shall bruise (or, lie in wait for) thy head, and thou shalt bruise (or, lie in wait for) his heel."[3] Whether this is history or allegory (and in my opinion it is certainly allegory), and whether it was written in the time of Moses or in that of Ezra, it is a Divinely-inspired prophecy—"the seed of the woman" is the Christ,

---

[1] Isaiah xix. 22, 24, 25.   [2] Psalm xc. 3.

[3] Gen. iii. 15. The meaning is the same whether we translate "bruise" or "lie in wait for" (see the margin of the Revised Version); lying in wait must be in order to attack and to wound.

and the mention of the wounded heel is a prophecy that the Christ should suffer. There are, it is true, suffering gods in some heathen mythologies; but though divine, they are regarded as finite and of limited power. The thought of a Messiah wounded and suffering in the strife, while vanquishing, trampling down, and destroying his enemies, was, on the contrary, too alien from Israelite feeling for any prophet or poet to utter, unless by Divine inspiration. And the mention of the Serpent's head is a prophecy that in the strife with the Messiah he shall be utterly destroyed, with all his works. A serpent, like any other vertebrate animal, is killed when its head is crushed or cut off; and all the activity of the power of evil, since Christ died "to destroy him that had the power of death,"[1] has been but the death-struggle of the Serpent.

We now go on to the prophecies of final restoration in the New Testament. Peter, the foremost of the Apostles in proclaiming forgiveness to those Jews of Jerusalem who had clamoured for the Saviour's death, spoke of "the Christ who hath been appointed for you, even Jesus; whom the Heaven must receive until the times of restoration of all things, whereof God spake by the mouth of all His holy prophets which have been since the world began."[2] "The restoration of all things" can only mean their restoration to sinless perfection and to the favour of God.

[1] Heb. ii. 14.   [2] Acts iii. 20, 21.

But the language of the Apostle of the Gentiles, though it could scarcely be clearer, is stronger and more emphatic. The earliest of his prophecies which I shall quote, is from that passage, the most eloquent ever written even by Divine inspiration, which has become associated with all our hopes of immortality:

"Now hath Christ been raised from the dead, the firstfruits of them that are asleep. For since by man came death, by man came also the resurrection of the dead. For as in Adam all die, so also in Christ shall all be made alive. But each in his own order: Christ the firstfruits; then they that are Christ's, at his coming. Then the end, when he shall deliver up the kingdom to God, even the Father; when he shall have abolished all rule and all authority and power. For he must reign until he hath put all enemies under his feet. The last enemy that shall be abolished is death. For, he put all things in subjection under his feet. But when he saith, All things are put in subjection, it is evident that he is excepted who did subject all things unto him. And when all things have been subjected unto him, then shall the Son also Himself be subjected to him that did subject all things unto him, that God may be all in all."[1]

"Note, that the same word is used of Christ's own subjection to the Father, and of the subjection of Christ's own enemies to Him. But, obviously, Christ's own subjection (to the Father) can only be

[1] 1 Cor. xv. 20, 28.

love and harmony."[1] So Saint Paul here not obscurely asserts that the subjection of His vanquished enemies to Christ is a subjection of the same kind—not of unwilling servitude, but of willing obedience. It would be difficult to assert the universality of salvation for mankind more clearly than Saint Paul has asserted it in this passage: "As in Adam all die, so also in Christ shall all be made alive." This is more than a prophecy of what is called in modern language, though not in the language of Holy Scripture, a resurrection to a future life. Life, in the language of the New Testament, when it has any higher meaning than merely natural life, never means life apart from God—it never means existence in Hades or Gehenna; and if such a meaning were possible in any context, it would be here excluded by the final words, "God shall be all in all."

The word death, also, in such a context as this, must be understood to mean not the death of the body merely, but the collective consequences of sin, which are spiritual death. See Saint Paul's expression elsewhere: "Awake, thou that sleepest, and arise from the dead, and Christ shall shine upon thee."[2] Respecting "the abolition of death," compare the following from Saint Paul's latest epistle: "Our Saviour Christ Jesus, who abolished death, and brought life and immortality to light through the Gospel";[3] and from the Epistle to the Hebrews, "That

---

[1] Allin's *Universalism Asserted*, p. 241.
[2] Eph. v. 14.   [3] 2 Tim. i. 10.

through death He might abolish him that had the power of death, that is, the devil; and might deliver all them who through fear of death were all their lifetime subject to bondage."[1] Compare also Saint John's words: "To this end was the Son of God manifested, that He might destroy the works of the devil";[2] not only the devil, but his works with him.

The next passage to be quoted is from the Epistle to the Romans. I italicise some important words, and divide it into five short paragraphs, in order to show to the eye its emphatic reiteration.

"As through one man sin entered into the world, and death through sin; and so death passed unto all men, for that all sinned: for until the law sin was in the world; but sin is not imputed when there is no law. Nevertheless death reigned from Adam until Moses, even over them that had not sinned after the likeness of Adam's transgression, who is a figure of him that was to come. But not as the trespass, so also is the free gift. For if by the trespass of the one *the many* died, *much more* did the grace of God, and the gift of the grace of the one man Jesus Christ, abound unto *the many*.

"And not as through one that sinned, so is the gift; for the judgment came of *one*, unto condemna-

---

[1] Heb. ii. 14, 15. The same word—καταργεῖν—is here, in the Revised Version, translated by *bring to nought*, and in the previously-quoted passages by *abolish*.

[2] 1st Epistle of John iii. 8.

tion, but the free gift came of *many* offences unto justification.

"For if, by the trespass of the one, death reigned through the one; *much more* shall they that receive the abundance of grace and of the gift of righteousness reign in life through the one, even Jesus Christ. So then as through one trespass the judgment came unto *all men* to condemnation; even so through one act of righteousness the free gift came unto *all men* to justification of life.

"For as through the one man's disobedience *the many* were made sinners, even so through the obedience of the one shall *the many* be made righteous.

"And the law came in beside, that the trespass might abound; but where sin *abounded*, grace did *abound more exceedingly*; that *as sin reigned in death, even so might grace reign* through righteousness *unto eternal life* through Jesus Christ our Lord."[1]

Language could not assert more clearly and emphatically that the grace of God is co-extensive with man's need, and more abundant than man's sin.

Saint Paul's later epistles teach the same doctrine as clearly, though not at equal length. In that to the Ephesians he says: "That in the dispensation of the fulness of times He might gather together in one all things in Christ, both which are in heaven and which are on earth."[2] And in that to the Colossians: "It was the good pleasure of the Father

---

[1] Romans v. 12, 21.   [2] Eph. i. 10.

that in him should all the Fulness (of the Godhead) dwell; and through him to reconcile all things unto himself, having made peace through the blood of his cross;—through him, I say, whether things upon the earth or things in the heavens."[1] Heaven and earth, in the language of the Epistles, are the names for the entire universe, invisible and visible, spiritual and material;[2] so that the Apostle here asserts that there is a work of reconciliation to be done by the Atonement of Christ among, and for, not only the inhabitants of earth, but also those of the spiritual world. This is a distinct contradiction of the doctrine that Christ's work of grace and salvation for men is limited to the present earthly dispensation.

The Epistle to the Philippians contains a still more remarkable expression of the same truth: "Our citizenship is in heaven; from whence also we wait for a Saviour, the Lord Jesus Christ; who shall fashion anew the body of our humiliation, that it may be conformed to the body of His glory, according to the working whereby He is able to subject all things unto Himself."[3] "The working whereby He is able to subject all things to Himself" might mean

[1] Col. i. 19, 20.

[2] See, besides the two passages last quoted, Colossians i. 16; Hebrews ix. 23, and xii. 26, 27; and Ephesians vi. 12. The last is especially remarkable; the mention of "the spiritual hosts of wickedness in the heavenly places" shows that heaven cannot be merely a synonym for the dwelling-place of God and the holy angels. Compare the prologue to Job.

[3] Philip. iii. 20, 21. For all that is implied in this subjection, see the remarks on 1 Cor. xv. 27, 28 (pp. 90, 91).

only resistless power; but we are here told that it is the same working whereby He will glorify our present mortality, which is sown in dishonour, to be raised in glory; sown in weakness, to be raised in power.[1] This is not wrought by mere Omnipotence; it has pleased God to work it by that "strength made perfect in weakness" which condescended to the Cross: and Saint Paul elsewhere tells us that if we are united with Christ in resurrection, it is because we have been united with Him in death.[2] Compare Christ's saying: "I, if I be lifted up from the earth, will draw all men unto myself. This He said, signifying by what death He should die."[3] It must be for salvation that Christ thus designed to draw all men unto Himself; He had no need to be lifted up on a cross in order to force them to Himself for judgment.

The next quotation is from one of Saint Paul's latest writings: "We have our hope set on the living God, who is the Saviour of all men, specially of them that believe."[4] This is rather strangely expressed, but it appears to declare that the condemnation of those who do not believe is not absolute or final. It is the same teaching as that of the classical passage: all shall be saved and made alive, but not all at first—"each in his own order." Compare the words of Christ to Nicodemus: "God so loved the world that He gave his only begotten Son, that

[1] 1 Cor. xv. 43.
[2] Rom. vi. 5, 8.
[3] John xii. 32, 33.
[4] 1 Tim. iv. 10.

whosoever believeth on Him should not perish, but have eternal life. For God sent not the Son into the world to condemn the world; but that *the world* should be saved through Him."[1] That is to say, salvation and eternal life are to be conferred first on the elect, the believers of the present dispensation, but ultimately on the entire world of men.

I have next to quote from that very remarkable passage towards the end of the Epistle to the Romans, where Saint Paul speaks of the future of Israel and its effect on the destiny of the entire human race.

"Did they (of Israel) stumble that they might fall? God forbid; but by their fall salvation is come unto the Gentiles, for to provoke them (of Israel) to jealousy. Now if their fall is the riches of the world, and their loss the riches of the Gentiles, how much more their fulness? . . .

"For if the casting away of them is the reconciling of the world, what shall the receiving of them be but life from the dead? And if the firstfruit is holy, so is the lump; and if the root is holy, so are the branches. . . .

"A hardening in part hath befallen Israel, until the fulness of the Gentiles be come in; and so all Israel shall be saved. . . . As touching the Gospel they (of Israel) are enemies for your sake; but as touching the election, they are beloved for the fathers'

[1] John iii. 16 17.

sake. For the gifts and calling of God are not repented of. For as ye in time past were disobedient to God, but have now obtained mercy through their disobedience, even so have these also now been disobedient, that by the mercy shown to you they also may now obtain mercy. For God hath shut up all unto disobedience, that He may have mercy upon all.

"O the depth of the riches both of the wisdom and the knowledge of God! how unsearchable His judgments, and how untraceable [1] His ways! ... For of Him, and through Him, and unto Him, are all things." [2]

Before we consider this passage taken altogether, let us inquire the meaning of the 16th verse: "If the firstfruit is holy, so is the lump; and if the root is holy, so are the branches." Are these two metaphors identical in meaning? Is this verse an instance of parallelism, like that of Hebrew poetry? The meaning of the second clause admits of no doubt; the following verses show that the root is the Patriarchs, and the branches are the people of Israel; so that this is a metaphorical equivalent of the 28th verse: "As touching the election, they are beloved for the fathers' sake." But I would suggest that the former of the two metaphors has a different meaning; that the "lump" is the human race, and the "firstfruit" the elect Israel, the seed of Abraham, who were

---

[1] Ἀνεξιχνίαστος, from ἴχνος, a footstep.
[2] Rom. xi. 11-36.

chosen to be not only holy and blessed themselves, but a blessing to all the nations of the earth. This interpretation is suggested by the mention, in the previous verse, of the world at large being blessed through Israel: "If the casting away of them be the reconciling of the world, what shall the receiving of them be but life from the dead?" And this is consistent with Saint Paul's use of the same metaphor elsewhere: "Christ the firstfruits; afterward they that are Christ's at His coming."[1] Moreover, the same metaphor is used with the same meaning by Saint James, who had much in common with Saint Paul, and was the author of that circular letter which was the charter of Christian freedom and equality to the Gentile Churches.[2] He says: "Of His own will begat He us by the word of truth, that we should be a kind of firstfruits of His creatures."[3] If this is the right interpretation of Saint Paul's allusion to the firstfruit in the passage which we are considering, the entire verse means: "Mankind is holy for the sake of the elect Church, even as Israel is holy and beloved (see verse 28) for the sake of the fathers."[4] But whether or not this interpretation is admitted for this passage, there appears no danger of error in uniting the verse quoted from Saint James with that from

---

[1] 1 Cor. xv. 23.   [2] Acts xv. 13 *et seq.*   [3] James i. 18.
[4] Since the above was written I have noticed, with much pleasure, that the same interpretation is offered by the Rev. Andrew Jukes, in *The Restitution of all Things*, p. 102. See Note A at end of chapter.

Saint Paul, and reading on from the one to the other, thus: "He begat us, that we should be a kind of firstfruits of His creatures. And if the firstfruit is holy, so is the lump." Westcott says, commenting on another passage: "It is through the fulfilment of His work for the Church—the firstfruits—that (Christ) moves towards the fulfilment of His work for the world."[1]

In the interpretation of the entire chapter before us, the chief problem is to determine of what the Apostle is speaking, and especially of whom he speaks when he declares that at the last "all Israel shall be saved." Who are the Israel spoken of? Is Israel here merely a synonym for the elect people of God, and is this simply a declaration that none of the sheep of Christ shall perish, neither shall any one be able to tear them out of His Father's hand?[2] This no doubt is true; but the connection of this verse with what precedes and what follows, shows that such is not the Apostle's thought in the present passage. He is speaking of Israel as a nation; and the entire passage is a declaration that as the rejection of the Christ by the Israelite people has led to the proclamation of the Gospel to the Gentiles, so the mercy now extended to the Gentiles will in the fulness of time be the means of bringing back Israel to the fold of God, and the entire nation will become obedient to God in Christ.

But is this all? What of those "whose carcasses

---

[1] Westcott on *Hebrews*, p. 230.   [2] John x. 28.

fell in the wilderness"?[1] What has the Apostle to say of his brethren according to the flesh who were resisting the Saviour, and of whom he saw that the wrath was coming upon them to the uttermost?[2] Had he regarded God's government from the point of view of the books of Moses, the question would scarcely have arisen; the blessings of the Mosaic dispensation were national blessings; and though the generation which came out of Egypt with Moses died in the wilderness, yet the nation of Israel entered into the Promised Land. But could such a hope as this satisfy Saint Paul, whose whole mind was dominated by the thoughts of the resurrection of the dead, Christ's future judgment of mankind, and eternal life? When he said that all Israel shall be ultimately saved, is it possible that he only meant to say that every Israelite who lives in the last times shall be saved, but the generations who have rejected Christ have died without hope? The rejection of Christ by his fellow-Israelites, he tells us, caused him "great sorrow and unceasing pain in his heart;"[3] and was there no consolation for this, except the thought of a salvation in the indefinitely remote future, from which they were to be excluded whom he had known on earth—his fellow-students at Jerusalem, his playmates at Tarsus, his kinsmen according to the flesh, one of whom, apparently not a Christian believer, afterwards saved

---

[1] Hebrews iii. 17.   [2] 1 Thess. ii. 16.
[3] Romans ix. 1, 2.

his life at Jerusalem?¹ Were those to remain under the wrath of God for ever? This is not what he teaches. He asserts that the Israelites who have rejected Christ are to receive mercy at last. "God hath shut up all unto disobedience, that He may have mercy upon all." And the answer for Gentiles is the same as the answer for Jews. If salvation is universal for the one, it is universal for the other.

It is, however, very generally believed that in the Synoptic Gospels our Lord teaches the opposite of this; namely, that for the rejected of the present dispensation there is no hope whatever; not even a hope that the vengeance which follows their sins, may end their sufferings by ending their existence. It is true that some of His sayings admit of this interpretation; perhaps, in view of the fact that such has been the prevailing belief of all branches of the Western Church from the time of Augustin until our own, we must admit that it is their most obvious interpretation. But, as we have seen, the obvious and superficial interpretation is not always the true.

The classical passage respecting judgment is the description by Our Lord of His future judgment of all nations,² when the merciful shall be rewarded with eternal life, and the unmerciful punished in eternal fire. But it cannot be meant as a full account of the final destiny of man, because it says nothing of the forgiveness of sins; yet this is a

[1] Acts xxiii. 16 *et seq.*   [2] Matt. xxv. 31 *et seq.*

characteristic and fundamental doctrine of Our Lord. It has been generally believed that in this passage "eternal" means absolutely endless, that "punishment" means mere vengeance, and that fire means nothing more than the infliction of the intensest pain. But none of these interpretations can be sustained.

The word αἰώνιος, which is translated by eternal, is derived from αἰών, an age, which signifies a time of limited duration; especially, in the New Testament, the period of the present world or the present dispensation; as in the expression, "the harvest is the end of the world,"[1] where the exact translation, given in the margin of the Revised Version, is "the consummation of the age." αἰώνιος is an indefinite word; in most places it means only *agelong*; and there is at least one passage in the New Testament where it is definitely used of time which, so far from being endless, has already come to an end: "The revelation of the mystery which has been kept in silence through *times eternal*, but now is manifested; and by the Scriptures of the Prophets, according to the commandment of the *eternal God*, is made known unto all the nations unto obedience of faith."[2] Here the word eternal is used twice; being in the one place applied to the times which ended with the coming of Christ, and in the other to Him who "hath immortality" by His essential nature. In

---

[1] Matt. xiii. 39.
[2] Rom. xvi. 25, 26. See also 2 Tim. i. 9, and Titus i. 2, for the expression "before times eternal."

view of this use of the word, it cannot be maintained that the eternal punishment denounced and the eternal life promised, in Our Lord's description of the Judgment, are necessarily of equal duration.

In that description of the Judgment, alone in the Old and New Testaments, is eternal punishment mentioned; and eternal destruction ($\ὄλεθρος$) is also mentioned once, and only once.[1] It is, however, remarkable, and cannot be without significance, that although eternal life is often mentioned in Holy Scripture, there is no mention of eternal death; the use of this expression is carefully avoided, even where it appears to be required for the symmetry of the sentence. I quote the following, italicising some important words:

"He that soweth to the flesh shall of the flesh reap *corruption*, but he that soweth to the Spirit shall of the Spirit reap *eternal life*."[2]

"To them that by patient continuance in well-doing seek for glory and honour and immortality, *eternal life*; but unto them that are factious, and obey not the truth, but obey unrighteousness, *wrath and indignation, tribulation and anguish*, upon every soul of man that worketh evil; but glory and honour and peace to every man that worketh good."[3]

"That as sin reigned in *death*, even so might grace reign through righteousness unto *eternal life* through Jesus Christ our Lord."[4]

[1] 2 Thess. i. 9.   [2] Gal. vi. 8.   [3] Rom. ii. 7-10.
[4] Rom. v. 21.

"What fruit had ye then in those things whereof ye are now ashamed? for the end of those things is *death*. But now being made free from sin, and become servants to God, ye have your fruit unto holiness, and the end *eternal life*. For the wages of sin is *death*, but the gift of God is *eternal life*, through Jesus Christ our Lord."[1]

We have next to consider the meaning of the word which is translated by *punishment* in Our Lord's account of the Judgment. That word is κόλασις. It does not mean vengeance or purely retributive punishment (for which the Greek word is τιμωρία); its etymological signification is pruning, whence it has come in classical Greek to mean chastisement or disciplinary correction. It is no doubt conceivable that in Hellenistic Greek κόλασις might have so far changed its meaning as to signify mere vengeance, somewhat as punishment in vulgar English has come to signify mere pain; but this would be contrary to the use of the word in the only other place in the New Testament where it occurs. This is as follows: "There is no fear in love; but perfect love casteth out fear, because fear hath punishment; he that feareth is not made perfect in love."[2] The fear and punishment which are incompatible with perfect love, but (as the

---

[1] Rom. vi. 21-23.

[2] 1st Epistle of John, iv. 18. The Authorised Version has *torment* where the Revised has *punishment*, but it needs no knowledge of Greek to see the inappropriateness of this.

Apostle evidently means) quite compatible with love growing to perfection, can have no mixture of vengeance, but must be purely disciplinary and corrective. When thus we see that κόλασις in its etymology, and generally in classical Greek, means not vengeance but correction or chastisement, and that in one of the two places where it occurs in the New Testament it unquestionably retains its original meaning, it appears all but certain that in the other place its meaning must be the same.

It appears, then, that the true meaning of κόλασις αἰώνιος is "agelong chastisement." This is strongly confirmed by another remarkable choice of words in the passage under consideration. It begins as follows, quoting from the Revised Version, and adopting the marginal readings: "When the Son of Man shall come in his glory, and all the angels with him, then shall he sit on the throne of his glory; and before him shall be gathered all the nations: and he shall separate them one from another, as a shepherd separateth the sheep from the kids; and he shall set the sheep on his right hand, but the kids on the left." Goats, like sheep, are clean beasts, and both are in the flock; the goats are only less dear than the sheep to the Shepherd; and if Our Lord, who elsewhere calls Himself the Good Shepherd,[1] had regarded the condemned as fit for nothing but burning, He would have called them by some such name as wolves, or swine, or vipers. But

---

[1] John x. 14. See also Luke xv. 3-7; and Matt. xviii. 12.

not only this: while calling those who are saved sheep, He goes out of His way to call the condemned, not goats but kids, and, in the second place where the word occurs, kidlings (ἐρίφια)—a double diminutive. These are words of endearment, as diminutives generally are; and moreover they suggest immaturity; which, when mentioned in connection with sin, can be understood only as a palliative of guilt. The sketch in the Catacombs of Rome, representing Christ bearing a kid on His shoulders, appears to prove that this interpretation was known to the Primitive Church.[1]

We have now to consider the meaning of the fire denounced against sinners in this passage and in many other parts of Holy Scripture.

Fire has the property of causing intense pain; it destroys, and in destroying it purifies; it is an energy, and is the source of light and warmth and life. These its different properties are all included in the symbolism of Scripture, but in different places they are prominent in different degrees; and it appears doubtful whether pain is the predominant idea connected with it anywhere, except in the apologue of Dives and Lazarus, where Dives says, "I am in anguish in this flame."[2] But if pain were in general the predominant idea, there is no reason why the image of fire should be so constantly used; the scourge and the cross were more familiar to Our

---

[1] See Matthew Arnold's sonnet "The Good Shepherd with the Kid." [2] Luke xvi. 24.

Lord's contemporaries; yet the cross is never used as an image of future punishment, and the scourge only once, and that, moreover, in a way which at least strongly suggests that the punishment, however severe, is to be but for a time. "That servant, which knew his lord's will, and made not ready, nor did according to his will, shall be beaten with many stripes; but he that knew not, and did things worthy of stripes, shall be beaten with few stripes."[1]

In the following passage, which beyond doubt contains Christ's teaching, though the words are those of John the Baptist, the thought of pain is not directly suggested, and the ideas of destruction and of purification are blended: "Even now is the axe laid unto the root of the trees; every tree therefore that bringeth not forth good fruit is hewn down and cast into the fire. I indeed baptize you in water unto repentance; but he that cometh after me is mightier than I; he shall baptize you in the Holy Spirit and in fire; whose winnowing-fan is in his hand, and he will thoroughly cleanse his threshing-floor, and he will gather his wheat into the garner, but the chaff he will burn up with unquenchable fire."[2] Here fire is mentioned together with the Holy Spirit, in a way which seems to imply that they are related as the symbol to that which is symbolised—an interpretation which is confirmed by the flames of fire in the miracle of Pentecost;[3]

---

[1] Luke xii. 47, 48. [2] Matt. iii. 10-12.
[3] Acts. ii. 3.

where, however, the thought of purification is subordinate to those of light and life and all-penetrating energy.

The same is in all probability the true meaning of another saying of Our Lord which has often been quoted to show the hopelessness of the future state; and we cannot deny that such is its obvious and superficial meaning. I quote from the revised translation of the revised text: "If thy hand cause thee to stumble, cut it off; it is good for thee to enter into life maimed, rather than having thy two hands to go into Gehenna, into the unquenchable fire. And if thy foot cause thee to stumble, cut it off; it is good for thee to enter into life halt, rather than having thy two feet to be cast into Gehenna. And if thine eye cause thee to stumble, cast it out; it is good for thee to enter into the kingdom of God with one eye, rather than having two eyes to be cast into Gehenna; where their worm dieth not, and the fire is not quenched. For every one shall be salted with fire."[1]

The mention of the worm and the fire is an allusion to the concluding words of the Book of Isaiah:[2] "They shall go forth, and look upon the carcasses of the men that have transgressed against

---

[1] Mark ix. 43 *et seq.*

[2] There is no special significance in the position of these words at the end of the book. The Book of Isaiah is little more of a unity than the Book of Psalms. It is different with the emphatic conclusion of such a book as, for instance, the Epistle of James, which is obviously and unquestionably a unity.

me : for their worm shall not die, neither shall their fire be quenched ; and they shall be an abhorring to all flesh." This is not a threat of torment, but of what many men fear as much, namely, the disgrace of bodies after death. Our Lord spiritualises the image ; in His application of it—if not, indeed, in the Prophet's original use of it—the worm represents the natural effects of sin, and the fire, the anger of God against sin. We do no violence to Christ's words if we understand them to mean that the worm will not die so long as anything is left for it to devour, and the fire will burn so long as anything is left for it to consume. Both the worm and the fire are destructive agents ; and we import into these passages a foreign, and, indeed, a self-contradictory meaning, if we maintain that the work of destruction goes on for ever, and is never accomplished. Isaiah's words suggest total destruction ending in extinction ; and such destruction is purification. But our Lord, in quoting Isaiah's words, drops a hint that while they are true, they are not the entire truth. He says, in allusion to the Levitical ritual of sacrifice, "For every one shall be salted with fire ; " suggesting that the fire of God's anger against sin will not only destroy the sin, but through that destruction will preserve and ultimately save the sinner. God can save, not only from the fire and through the fire,[1] but by means of the fire.

We conclude, then, that the fire, which is the

[1] 1 Cor. iii. 15.

symbol both of the Holy Spirit of blessing and of the Divine anger against sin, will not only punish sin, but will in punishing destroy it; and by destroying the sin will purify the sinner, and make him fit for the kingdom of God.

The possibility of salvation in a future life is hinted at also in these words of Our Lord: "Agree with thine adversary quickly, whilst thou art with him in the way: lest the adversary deliver thee to the judge, and the judge deliver thee to the officer, and thou be cast into prison. Verily I say unto thee, Thou shalt by no means come out thence till thou have paid the last farthing."[1] The "adversary" appears to be conscience personified; but the interpretation of this expression does not affect the meaning of the final clause, "till thou have paid the last farthing." This has been interpreted to mean that the imprisonment can never end, because it will never be possible for man to pay the debt which by his sins he has incurred to God. Such an interpretation violates no rule of grammar or logic, but it cannot be Our Lord's meaning. He often uttered the most passionate denunciations, and once at least he gave utterance to indignant irony: "Full well ($καλῶς$) do we reject the commandment of God, that ye may keep your tradition";[2] but the irony implied in this interpretation—not indignant, but cold, cruel, and sneering—is totally unlike anything in His words or His character.

[1] Matt. v. 25, 26.   [2] Mark vii. 9.

The same doctrine of the possibility of forgiveness and reconciliation in a future life for those who pass out of the present life unforgiven and unreconciled, is suggested under the same image, but even more distinctly, in the following passage: "The kingdom of heaven is likened unto a king which would make a reckoning with his servants. And one was brought unto him which owed him ten thousand talents (about two millions and a half sterling). But forasmuch as he had not wherewith to pay, his lord commanded him to be sold, and his wife and children and all that he had, and payment to be made."[1] Every word of Our Lord's is significant, and the concluding statement of the parable that payment *was to be made* at the debtor's expense, is altogether inconsistent with a never-ending imprisonment. The evident meaning of this, as of the previous passage quoted, is that salvation will be possible in the future life, but on harder terms than in the present.

The final restoration of all is also strongly suggested in our Lord's two parables of the Lost Sheep and the Lost Coin: "What man of you, having a hundred sheep and having lost one of them, doth not leave the ninety and nine in the wilderness and go after that which is lost, until he find it? . . .

---

[1] Matt. xviii. 23-25. The servants were evidently governors of provinces, and the debts were tribute, for the punctual collection and remittance of which the governors were responsible.

Or what woman, having ten pieces of silver, if she lose one piece, doth not light a lamp, and sweep the house, and seek diligently until she find it?"[1] There is no suggestion, in either of these parables, of any possibility that what was lost may not be found. It is true that in the parallel passage in Matthew[2] the words occur, "if so be that he find it"; this, however, cannot be meant to suggest that Christ's search for the lost sheep may after all be unsuccessful; but rather to suggest that if the rescue of a lost sheep by a human shepherd is possible, its rescue by the Divine Shepherd is certain. With this agrees His saying: "The Son of Man came to seek and to save that which was lost."[3]

If we are reminded that not all men are Christ's sheep,[4] we reply that this is true under the present dispensation; but all things, in both the visible and the invisible worlds, have been given by the Father to Christ. "All things have been delivered unto me of my Father."[5] "All authority hath been given unto me in heaven and on earth."[6] And in yet clearer words He elsewhere tells for what purpose all things have been given to Him. In His "consecration prayer," as it has been well called, He says: ἔδωκας αὐτῷ ἐξουσίαν πάσης σαρκός, ἵνα πᾶν ὃ δέδωκας αὐτῷ, δώσῃ αὐτοῖς ζωὴν αἰώνιον. That is, literally translated, "Thou gavest Him authority over ALL

---

[1] Luke xv. 4, 8. [2] Matt. xviii. 13. [3] Luke xix. 10.
[4] John x. 26. [5] Matt. xi. 27. [6] Matt. xxviii. 18.

flesh, that ALL which Thou hast given Him, He should give to them eternal life."[1]

Our review of the teaching of Holy Scripture respecting the fate of the rejected of the present dispensation would be imcomplete and unsatisfactory if we were to omit the Apocalypse, which I believe to be the work of the Beloved Disciple, and rightly admitted into the canon of Scripture. Its testimony on the present subject is more than usually uncertain and apparently contradictory. The following passage is in this respect typical of the entire book. I italicise some words :

"I heard a great voice out of the throne, saying, Behold, the tabernacle of God is with men, and he shall dwell with them, and they shall be his people, and God himself shall be with them, and shall be their God; and he shall wipe away every tear from their eyes; and *death shall be no more: neither shall there be mourning, nor crying, nor pain any more; the first things are passed away.* And he that sitteth on the throne said, *Behold, I make all things new.* . . . He that overcometh shall inherit these things; I will be his God, and he shall be my son. But for the fearful, and unbelieving, and abominable, and murderers, and fornicators, and sorcerers, and

---

[1] John xvii. 2. Both the Authorised and the Revised Versions miss the significance of this passage by not repeating the emphatic word *all*. It is pointed out in Allin's *Universalism Asserted*, pp. 230, 231.

idolaters, and all liars, *their part shall be in the lake that burneth with fire and brimstone; which is the second death.*"[1]

When we meet with such a contradiction as this, the right way to resolve it is by the principle expressed by Saint Paul, that the ministration of condemnation is indeed glorious, yet it passeth away; but the ministration of righteousness excelleth in glory, and remaineth.[2] In the same spirit, Isaiah asserts that wrath and vengeance are strange to God, though they may be forced on Him. "The Lord shall rise up, he shall be wroth; that he may do his work, his strange work; and bring to pass his act, his strange act."[3]

Still more difficult, if read without their context, are the following words, also from the Apocalypse: "He that is unrighteous, let him do unrighteousness still; and he that is filthy let him be made filthy still; and he that is righteous let him do righteousness still; and he that is holy let him be made holy still."[4] This has been often quoted as an assertion of the unchangeableness of man's moral nature in the future state, and the consequent impossibility of repentance and forgiveness. But it is not spoken of the future state; it is spoken before the judgment, as is shown by the following words: "Behold, I come quickly, and my reward is with me, to render to each man according as his work is." If

---

[1] Rev. xxi. 3-8. [2] 2 Cor. iii. 6-11.
[3] Isaiah xxviii. 21. [4] Rev. xxii. 11.

this passage were understood according to its most obvious meaning, it would be a denial of the possibility of repentance in the present life. It is, however, only a statement of that law under which evil is punished by its own increase, and goodness rewarded in the same way; and what makes it seem strange is the use of the imperative where the sense would appear to require the indicative; but this has parallels elsewhere in Scripture, especially in a well-known passage of Isaiah, where a prophecy is expressed as a command: "Hear ye indeed but understand not, and see ye indeed but perceive not. Make the heart of this people fat, and make their ears heavy, and shut their eyes; lest they see with their eyes, and hear with their ears, and understand with their heart, and turn again and be healed."[1] This substitution of the imperative for the indicative is a Hebraism, though rather of thought than of grammar.

When we are asked, In what passage of Holy Scripture are we taught that repentance and forgiveness are possible in a future life? it would be enough to answer, In what passage are we taught that they are impossible? where has God said that He has put it out of His own power to follow with His mercy the sinner across the barrier of death? But He has expressly taught, through His Apostle Peter, that it is not impossible; that the barrier

[1] Isaiah vi. 9, 10.

may be passed. "Christ also suffered for sins once, the righteous for the unrighteous, that He might bring us to God; being put to death in the flesh, but made alive in the spirit; in which also He went and preached unto the spirits in prison, which aforetime were disobedient, when the longsuffering of God waited in the days of Noah, while the Ark was a preparing."[1] "Who shall give account to Him that is ready to judge the living and the dead. For unto this end were the good tidings preached even to the dead, that they might be judged according to men in the flesh, but live according to God in the spirit."[2] I do not fully understand these passages—probably no one does; but they are conclusive as to the Apostle's belief that death is no barrier to the mercy of God.

It is true that there are passages in the New Testament which, taken alone, appear to teach that there are sins which cannot be forgiven. Saint John speaks of a sin which is unto death, and sins which are not unto death.[3] And Our Lord says: "Whosoever shall speak a word against the Son of Man it shall be forgiven him (not *may*, but *shall*); but whosoever shall speak against the Holy Spirit it shall not be forgiven him, neither in this age nor in that which is to come."[4] Or, as reported by another Evangelist: "All their sins shall be forgiven unto the sons of men, and all blasphemies wherewith-

---

[1] 1 Peter iii. 18-20. [2] 1 Peter iv. 5, 6.
[3] 1st Epistle of John v. 16. [4] Matt. xii. 32.

soever they shall blaspheme; but whosoever shall blaspheme against the Holy Spirit hath not forgiveness for ever, but is guilty of an eternal sin."[1] And the Epistle to the Hebrews teaches the same even more emphatically: "If we sin wilfully after we have received the knowledge of the truth, there remaineth no more a sacrifice for sins, but a certain fearful expectation of judgment, and a fierceness of fire which shall devour the adversaries."[2] This passage explains Christ's saying: the sin against the Holy Spirit is sin against light, and abuse of religious privileges. Christ says that all other sins not only may be, but shall be, forgiven.

Now the sins of unmercifulness against which, in the parable of the Sheep and the Goats, Our Lord threatens punishment in eternal fire, are not of the unpardonable class; for they have not been committed by those who, in the language of the Epistle to the Hebrews, "were once enlightened."[3] This is shown by their question: "When saw we thee hungered, or athirst, or a stranger, or naked, or sick, or in prison, and ministered not unto thee?" Christ's prayer for His executioners, "Father, forgive them, for they know not what they do," is for such as these, and shall be granted for them. The parable of the Sheep and the Goats represents the judgment of the world; the parables of the Virgins and of the Talents represent respectively the judg-

---

[1] Mark iii. 28, 29 (Revised Version).
[2] Hebrews x. 26, 27.   [3] Hebrews vi. 4.

ment of the Church and of the Ministry.[1] Roman soldiers and other sinners of the outside world, who have known God and Christ only afar off if at all, have had no opportunity of sinning against the Holy Spirit of Light; but Christ gave warning against that sin among Israelites, and the writer to the Hebrews gives warning against the same among Christians.

But what are we to believe of the destiny of those who have committed that sin? The words of the writer to the Hebrews, taken alone, appear to leave no hope except of annihilation: "No more a sacrifice for sins, but a fierceness of fire which shall devour the adversaries."[2] But we have the words of Christ: "I, if I be lifted up (on the cross), shall draw all men unto myself (for salvation)"; and of Saint Paul, that God, through Christ, will reconcile all things to Himself.

When I wrote my *Scientific Bases of Faith* twenty years ago, I leaned to the opinion that for those who sin against the Holy Spirit there is no resurrection from the death of sin, and no hope except the hope of annihilation. I now "faintly trust the larger hope"[3] for all, without any exception; for it does not appear impossible that those who cannot be forgiven in either this life or the next may be forgiven in some far-off age. Of this, however, we may be certain, that if any sins are beyond forgive-

---

[1] Matt. xxv.   [2] See, however, Note B at end of chapter.
[3] *In Memoriam*.

ness, it is because they have passed too deeply into character for repentance.

Besides the testimony of Holy Scripture there are two moral arguments—not perhaps for absolutely universal restoration, but certainly against the hopelessness of the future state—which are of great and, to me, conclusive force.

In the first place, granting—what I do not grant—that the perfecting of an elect Church is the last word and the ultimate purpose of Creation, Providence, and Grace, it will even then be best for the elect that their hopes should not be selfish, but that they should look forward to sharing their bliss with all. This argument is based on general and recognised facts of human nature. But I will add that, for myself, a belief in the hopelessness of the future state—a conviction that eternal hope was baseless—would make any feeling of thankfulness towards God impossible.

The second argument is drawn from the treatment by God of men's religious aspirations under the dispensation of the Old Testament. The perplexity of the faithful of old—those men whose historical types are David, Asaph, and Job—was that God should permit iniquity to prosper and triumph; and God's revealed reply was, that it shall not be so for ever; that all powers of iniquity shall be overtaken by the vengeance of God. But to the Christian this answer is only too complete; he knows that it is worse for the man who inflicts wrong than for the man who suffers wrong; and with him the perplexity is that God should permit sin and suffering to exist at all. Now, when the perplexity of the Israelite has been cleared away by the revelation that it shall not be so for ever; and when—chiefly in consequence of this very revelation—the more deeply spiritual mind of the Christian has awakened to a deeper difficulty which the Israelite did not feel; it is impossible to believe that He who is the same yesterday, to-day, and for ever, who answered the Israelite by declaring that the triumph of iniquity *shall not* continue without end, should answer the perplexity of the Christian by declaring that the existence of sin and suffering *shall* continue without end.

NOTE A.

THE "FIRSTFRUITS" AND THE "FIRSTBORN."

IN reference to the remarks on the doctrine of the "firstfruits" on pages 97-99, I have much pleasure in speaking with unqualified praise of *The Second Death and the Restitution of all Things*, by the Rev. Andrew Jukes, especially that part of the work which treats of the typical and symbolic system of the Mosaic law—a subject on which I say scarcely anything, for the reason that I am conscious of not understanding it sufficiently. He lays down (page 30 *et seq.*) that it is "the purpose of God by the firstfruits, or firstborn, to save and bless the later born." The passages which I have quoted on the pages referred to are sufficient to show that this is the doctrine of Scripture. I will, however, here add the following :—

Christ is "the firstborn from the dead, that in all things He might have the pre-eminence;"[1] and the elect of the present dispensation are called "the general assembly and church of the firstborn who are enrolled in Heaven."[2] In symbolic language, "firstborn" is evidently a synonym of "firstfruits;" and the saying that "if the firstfruit is holy, so is the lump,"[3] is only translated into a kindred form of expression by saying that if the firstborn are holy, so is the race; the salvation of the "general assembly and church of the firstborn" is the firstfruit of the salvation of mankind.

NOTE B.

WESTCOTT ON UNPARDONABLE SIN.

THE writer to the Hebrews says (vi. 4-6), "As touching those who were once enlightened, and tasted of

---

[1] Col. i. 18.   [2] Heb. xii. 23.   [3] Rom. xi. 16.

the heavenly gift, and were made partakers of the Holy Spirit, and tasted the good word of God, and the powers of the age to come, and then fell away, it is impossible to renew them again unto repentance" (πάλιν ἀνακαινίζειν εἰς μετάνοιαν).

Westcott, in his *Epistle to the Hebrews: the Greek text, with Notes and Essays,* has the following note *in loco*:—"The use of the active voice limits the strict application of the words to human agency. This is all that comes within the range of the writer's argument. And further, the present (ἀνακαινίζειν) suggests continual effort. Some divine work may then be equivalent to this renewing, though not identical with it."

Westcott then refers to Our Lord's words, "With men this is impossible, but with God all things are possible" (Matt. xix. 26). Our Lord had said to the disciples, "It is easier for a camel to go through a needle's eye than for a rich man to enter into the Kingdom of God." They were naturally much astonished; for they knew that all men, as a rule, are subject to the temptations of riches—those who are not rich desire to be rich—and they said, "Who then can be saved?" Is salvation so much more difficult to attain than we thought? To which the Lord replied by telling them that salvation is not attainable by anything that man can do, but must be the work of God, with whom all things are possible.

Respecting the "sin unto death" mentioned by Saint John, of which he does *not* say that we should pray for its forgiveness when we see it committed by a fellow Christian (1st Epistle of John v. 16), Westcott, after speaking of sins which were capital under the Law of Moses, proceeds (*The Epistles of St. John: the Greek Text, with Notes and Essays*, p. 199 *et seq.*) :

"It was a natural extension of this meaning [of a "sin unto death"] when the phrase was used for an offence which was reckoned by moral judgment to belong to the same class.

"If now the same line of thought is extended to the Christian society, it will appear that a sin which by its very nature excludes from fellowship with Christians, would be rightly spoken of as a sin unto death. Such a sin may be seen in hatred of the brethren, or in the selfishness which excludes repentance, the condition of forgiveness, or in the faithlessness which denies Christ, the One Advocate. But in each case the character of the sin is determined by the effect which it has on the relation of the doer to God through Christ in the Divine society. We are not to think of specific acts, defined absolutely, but of acts as the revelation of moral life.

"It must be noticed further that St. John speaks of the sin as 'tending to death' ($\pi\rho\grave{o}s\ \theta\acute{a}\nu a\tau o\nu$), and not as necessarily involving death. Death is, so to speak, its natural consequence, if it continue, and not its inevitable issue as a matter of fact. Its character is assumed to be unquestionable, and its presence open and notorious.

"The question then could not but arise, How is

such flagrant sin in a brother—a fellow Christian—to be dealt with? For it must be remembered that the words of the Apostle are directed to those who are members of the Christian Church, sharing in the privileges of the common life. The answer follows naturally from a view of the normal efficacy of Christian intercession. The power of prayer avails for those who belong to the Body. But for those who are separated from the Body for a time, or not yet included in it, the ordinary exercise of the energy of spiritual sympathy has, so far as we are taught directly, no promise of salutary influence. The use of common prayer in such cases is not enjoined; though it must be observed that it is not forbidden. St. John does not command intercession when the sin is seen, recognised by the brother, in its fatal intensity; but on the other hand he does not expressly exclude it. Even if the tenour of his words may seem to dissuade such prayer, it is because the offender lies without the Christian Body, excluded from its life, but yet not beyond the creative, vivifying power of God.

"We can understand in some degree how such sins, either in men or in nations, must be left to God. Chastisement and not forgiveness is the one way to restoration. The book of the Prophet Jeremiah is a divine lesson of the necessity of purification through death for a faithless people. And the fortunes of Israel seems to illustrate the character of God's dealings with men."

CHAPTER VII.

RETRIBUTION AND FORGIVENESS.

I HAVE endeavoured to show in the foregoing chapter that we have every reason to hope for a "restoration of all things," in which sin and suffering shall cease to exist. But it is not true that forgiven sins are as though they had not been. On this subject, I quote the following passages from the prophetical writings; which, as is usual in both the Old and the New Testaments, state the apparently opposing truths of justice and mercy, retribution and forgiveness, without any hint to show how they are to be reconciled:—

"Jehovah is slow to anger and plenteous in mercy, forgiving iniquity and transgression, and will by no means clear the guilty."[1] "Thou wast a God that forgavest them, though Thou tookest vengeance of their doings."[2] These latter are the words of a Psalmist of the early Israelite Monarchy,

---

[1] Numbers xiv. 18; see also Exodus xxxiv. 7.
[2] Psalm xcix. 8.

perhaps of David himself, as he looked back on the troubled but glorious history of Israel from the departure out of Egypt to the establishment of the Kingdom in Zion: they assert that forgiveness is compatible with vengeance, and suggest, though they do not assert, that vengeance may be the way to forgiveness. And in the same spirit is that remarkable saying in the Psalm *De Profundis*, "There is forgiveness with Thee, that Thou mayest be feared."[1] But what is only suggested here is asserted in another psalm. "To Thee, O Lord, belongeth mercy: *for Thou renderest to every man according to his work.*"[2] Here the Psalmist, with a flash of inspired insight, has expressed the truth independently perceived by Plato, that it is good for the sinner to receive the reward of his deeds. This thought is expanded in the prayer of Solomon:—

"If there be in the land famine, if there be pestilence, if there be blasting or mildew, locust or caterpillar; if their enemies besiege them in the land of their cities; whatsoever plague or whatsoever sickness there be: what prayer and supplication soever be made by any man, or by all the people of Israel: . . . then hear Thou from Heaven Thy dwelling-place, and when Thou hearest, forgive, *and render unto every man according to his ways*, whose heart Thou knowest; for Thou, even Thou only, knowest the hearts of the children of men: that they may fear Thee, to walk in Thy ways."[3]

[1] Psalm cxxx. 4. [2] Psalm lxii. 12. [3] 2 Chron. vi. 28-31.

There is also a remarkable and seldom-quoted passage in the Prophecies of Ezekiel, where the Prophet teaches that those who truly repent of the sins which have alienated them from their God, and are converted, and assured of forgiveness and restoration, nevertheless cannot, will not, and ought not to think and feel about their sins as if they had not been committed :—

"Ye shall be my people, and I will be your God. And I will save you from your uncleannesses: and I will call for the corn, and will multiply it, and lay no famine upon you. And I will multiply the fruit of the tree, and the increase of the field, that ye shall receive no more the reproach of famine among the nations. Then shall ye remember your evil ways, and your doings that were not good; *and ye shall loathe yourselves in your own sight for your iniquities and your abominations.*" [1]

There is a still more remarkable passage in the same prophet, which carries the same lesson yet further: "The Levites that went far from Me, when Israel went astray, which went astray from Me after their idols; they shall bear their iniquity. Yet they shall be ministers in My sanctuary, having oversight at the gates of the house, and ministering in the house: they shall slay the burnt offering and the sacrifice for the people, and they shall stand before them to minister unto them. Because they ministered unto them before their idols, and became

[1] Ezek. xxxvi. 28-31; see also xx. 41-44.

a stumbling-block of iniquity unto the house of Israel; therefore have I lifted up My hand against them, saith the Lord God, and they shall bear their iniquity. And they shall not come near unto Me, to execute the office of priest unto Me, nor to come near to any of My holy things, unto the things that are most holy: *but they shall bear their shame, and their abominations which they have committed.* Yet will I make them keepers of the charge of the house, for all the service thereof, and for all that shall be done therein.

"But the priests, the Levites, the sons of Zadok, that kept the charge of My sanctuary when the children of Israel went away from Me, they shall come near to Me to minister unto Me, and they shall stand before Me to offer unto Me the fat and the blood, saith the Lord God: they shall enter into My sanctuary, and they shall come near to My table, to minister unto Me, and they shall keep My charge." [1]

We are here told that men who have sinned against the God whom they served, and have afterwards repented and been received back, may be permitted again to enter His service, though debarred from the highest service, which consists in ministering in His immediate presence:—that honour is reserved for those who have always remained faithful. I do not say that the Prophet wrote these words with immediate reference to the spiritual or

[1] Ezek. xliv. 10-16; see also xxxix. 25-27.

eternal world, but we cannot doubt that they have an eternal significance. The holy place made with hands was a type of the true, "the greater and more perfect tabernacle, not made with hands, that is to say, not of this creation."[1] The foregoing quotations from Ezekiel are from prophecies of the restoration of Israel from the exile in Babylon, and that restoration has always, I believe, been regarded by both Jews and Christians as a type of the ultimate salvation of the people of God in final bliss.

God has elsewhere said: "I will put My law in their inward parts, and in their heart will I write it: . . . for I will forgive their iniquity, and their sin will I remember no more."[2] And we are taught, not in the Prophecies of Jeremiah only, but throughout the Holy Scriptures, that when the sinner is truly converted through the law of God being written on his heart, God's forgiveness is absolute, so that He no longer remembers or accounts the sin against the sinner. Nothing less than this is meant by the saying in the earliest of the Christian Creeds: "I believe in the forgiveness of sins."[3] But a sinner who believes that he is forgiven by God cannot always forgive himself: and though the Divine

---

[1] Heb. ix. 11. [2] Jer. xxxi. 33-34.
[3] The Creeds (for the so-called Athanasian Creed is not a *credo*) contain no assertion of belief in the punishment of sins. This was taken for granted—just as they contain no assertion of belief in death, but do assert belief in the Resurrection. Punishment appeared as certain as death: Forgiveness and Resurrection needed an effort of faith to believe in them.

forgiveness cancels the severest part of the punishment of sin, which is the Divine anger, yet we know that in this present life it does not always, nor generally, destroy those secondary effects of sin which, by the operation of natural law, tend to make sin its own punishment; and there is no reason to believe that the law shall ever be repealed which ordains, "Whatsoever a man soweth, that shall he also reap."[1] We have no reason to think that he whose work is burned up in the fiery trial which, either in this life or in that which is to come, is to test every man's work,[2] shall ever attain to an equality with him whose work withstands the test. All punishment may, and I believe will, finally disappear as pain, but not as loss.

I go back to those passages from the Old Testament quoted above, which teach that God's mercy is revealed through justice, not by setting justice aside. It may be urged that they *are* from the Old Testament, and therefore belong to a dispensation which has been superseded by the fuller revelation of mercy in the Atonement of Christ. To this I give Saint Paul's reply, that the law is not made void, but on the contrary is confirmed, through the faith.[3] The Old Testament has made known the righteousness of God, with hints and foreshadowings of a further and profounder revelation of the same; the New Testament, taking this as known, reveals that God is not only Himself righteous, which He

---

[1] Gal. vi. 7.   [2] 1 Cor. iii. 10 *et seq.*   [3] Rom. iii. 31.

always was and cannot cease to be; but also, because He is righteous, has opened a way, through the Incarnation and Atonement of His Divine Son, whereby He can endow the sinful race of men with His own righteousness, on their submitting themselves to the Son in the obedence of faith.[1]

In the light of this revelation, then, it appears that the mercy of God flows naturally from His righteousness; that the purpose of the Atonement is not to make a separation between sin and punishment, but to destroy sin itself; and that the Divine forgiveness does not mean the remission of punishment, but the Eternal Father's purpose of mercy, which possibly may be best attained through punishment.[2]

[1] See Romans iii. 26.
[2] See Erskine's *Spiritual Order*, p. 140.

CHAPTER VIII.

THE LETTER AND THE SPIRIT.

[Part of the present chapter is reproduced from the article by the present writer, on "Christ's Use of Scripture," in the *Expositor* of August 1882.]

"The letter killeth, but the spirit giveth life." Few more significant words than these have ever been written; and when they were first written by Saint Paul they were absolutely new in expression, although the contrast between the spirit and the letter was implied by Jeremiah, when he foretold that God would make a new covenant with His people and write His laws in their heart;[1] and by Christ, when He began to fulfil that prophecy by dealing, as one having authority, with the laws of Moses; enlarging their scope, and proclaiming a dispensation of the Spirit, in which God required His people to serve Him not only in the life but in the heart, abstaining not only from sins of deed but from sins of thought.[2]

[1] Jer. xxxi. 33.   [2] Matt. v. 21 *et seq.*

CHAP. VIII *Saint Paul on the Letter and Spirit.* 133

The passage which contains the words quoted above, has even more than Saint Paul's usual involution of thought; and it may be a help to the understanding of it if we state its complex contrasts, retaining its words as nearly as possible, but in parallel columns, as follows :—

The Old Covenant, or Testament, is written on tables of stone, and is a ministration of the letter.	The New Covenant, or Testament, is written with the Spirit of the living God on tables that are hearts of flesh,[1] and is a ministration of the Spirit.
The letter killeth, and its ministration is a ministration of death and of condemnation, and passeth away.	The Spirit giveth life, and its ministration is a ministration of righteousness, and remaineth.
This ministration of the letter, of death and of condemnation, is glorious, but has no glory in comparison with the glory that surpasseth.	The surpassing glory of the ministration of the Spirit, of life, and of righteousness, makes the ministration of the letter, of death, and of condemnation, appear no longer glorious.

---

[1] An allusion to Jeremiah xxxi. 31, 33, "I will make a new covenant with the house of Israel, and with the house of Judah. . . . I will put My law in their inward parts, and in their heart will I write it;" and to Ezekiel xi. 19, "I will take the stony heart out of their flesh, and will give them a heart of flesh."

We are here taught that condemnation is to be superseded and to pass away, but righteousness and grace are to endure. Although the language and the metaphors are different, the thoughts of the foregoing passage are nearly the same which the Apostle afterwards worked out in the earlier chapters of the Epistle to the Romans, namely, that the law alone is but a sentence of death, while the Gospel is a spiritual revelation, and brings life; and the Epistle to the Galatians is chiefly occupied with the kindred truth of the subordinate and preparatory character of the Law in relation to the Gospel. The same is taught, though from a different point of view, in that wonderful passage where the Apostle insists on the supreme worth and glory of Love or Charity; saying that Love is to endure through all eternity, while prophecy shall be merged in fulfilment, the revelation taught in language superseded by the vision of truth, and our earthly apparatus of knowledge, with the reasonings on which it is based, exchanged for immediate intuition.[1]

The same is true in a lower sphere. In education, the highest use of the letter is to guide us to the understanding of the spirit; the highest use of authority is to train us to be independent of authority. Though everything in Euclid is true, and it is better to receive Euclid's truths on his authority than to remain altogether ignorant of them, yet the man who believes them on Euclid's authority only is

[1] 1 Cor. xiii. 8.

no geometrician, and does not know them as they ought to be known. So in religious knowledge. It is well to believe that forgiveness is a duty because Christ has declared it, and to practise the duty because He has commanded it; but it is better to believe and to practise the duty because it is seen to be right. This is not to disparage the letter; on the contrary, the worth and the glory of the letter consist in its being a teacher and guide whereby to ascend to the spirit.

We have now to see how the superiority of the spirit to the letter, which Saint Paul asserts in theory, has been practically applied by Christ. Some of the Sadducees, who denied the Resurrection, put to Him the case of a woman who had been the wife of seven men successively, and asked whose wife would she be in the Resurrection. He replied as follows:—

"Ye do err, not knowing the scriptures, nor the power of God."[1] "The sons of this world marry, and are given in marriage: but they that are accounted worthy to attain to that world, and the Resurrection from the dead, neither marry, nor are given in marriage: for neither can they die any more: for they are equal unto the angels; and are sons of God, being sons of the Resurrection. But that the dead are raised, even Moses showed in the place concerning the Bush, when he called the Lord

[1] Matt. xxii. 29.

the God of Abraham, and the God of Isaac, and the God of Jacob. Now He is not the God of the dead, but of the living: for all live unto Him."[1]

In some of Christ's applications of Scripture, He claims for Himself a peculiar relation to it; as in that memorable discourse in the synagogue at Nazareth, where He announces the fulfilment of prophecy, and Himself as fulfilling it;[2] or in the Sermon on the Mount, where He claims for Himself authority to correct, to add to, or to supersede the laws of Moses. But in most instances where He quotes from the Scriptures He does not speak "with authority," as fulfilling a prophecy or making a revelation; but uses Scripture, as His disciples from Saint Paul downwards have constantly done, for enforcement and illustration of the truths on which He is insisting. The passage now under consideration belongs to the second of these two classes. Christ here claims for Himself no special relation to Scripture. He is not speaking "with authority," or making any new revelation. He is neither fulfilling the prophecies of Isaiah nor correcting the laws of Moses; He is telling His audience what they ought to have found in Moses for themselves.

In order fully to understand our Lord's drift in this discourse, we must remember that the Sadducees, to whom it was addressed, regarded the Prophets, as well as the Psalms and the other Hagiographa, as inferior in authority to the Books of Moses. Now it

---

[1] Luke xx. 34-38.   [2] Luke iv. 16-21.

is true that the five books ascribed to Moses do not contain a single distinct assertion of a resurrection or of immortality; and we may reasonably suppose that the Sadducees, when pressed with passages from the later Scriptures which do assert it—such as that from David, "I shall be satisfied, when I awake, with Thy likeness,"[1] or that from Job, "I know that my Redeemer liveth, and that He shall stand at the latter day upon the earth: and . . . from my flesh shall I see God;"[2] we may reasonably suppose, I say, that the Sadducees used to reply: "Those sayings are all from books of inferior authority; but show us any distinct assertion of the Resurrection in the Books of Moses, and we will believe it." To this thought of theirs, Christ replied by telling them that there is more in Scripture than the mere letter; and that if they had known how to read between the lines of Moses, they would have found the doctrine of immortality there.

The case of the seven brothers and the wife was probably imaginary—what lawyers call an A B case—and had perhaps been often used in order to puzzle Pharisees and throw ridicule on the Resurrection. We do not know what the Pharisaic answer was, but we may suppose that a Pharisee would have been ready with his reasons for awarding the wife in dispute to either the first or the last of her seven husbands. Christ, on the contrary, does not condescend to answer the question at all, but declares

---

[1] Psalm xvii. 15.   [2] Job xix. 25, 26.

that it is a foolish and unmeaning question which ought not to have been asked.

There is something strange in the words of His rebuke: "Ye do err, not knowing the Scriptures, nor the power of God." Not knowing the Scriptures! They were doubtless well acquainted with the letter of Scripture. And not knowing the power of God! They had never thought of doubting it; and, besides, what had the power of God to do with the question? These words must have seemed to them mere heated invective. But though they knew the letter of the Scriptures, they did not know the Scriptures aright; and though they had never doubted the power of God, they really, though unconsciously, disparaged it, by suggesting as possible that, if it were God's will to raise the dead, He could meet with any difficulty arising out of the rights of husbands.

The same answer may sometimes be appropriate still. It has been seriously maintained—maintained not by scoffers, but by believers—that the doctrine of the Resurrection implies the gathering together, at the voice of the Archangel and the trump of God, of all the atoms of matter which constituted the body of each individual man at the moment of his death, in order that out of them the resurrection bodies may be rebuilt. To such a needless and repulsive fancy as this we may reply in the words of our Lord and of Saint Paul, "Ye do err, not knowing the scriptures, nor the power of God."[1] "Thou sowest not

[1] Matt. xxii. 29.

the body that shall be ... it is raised a spiritual body."[1]

More remarkable still is the concluding sentence of Christ's reply, in which He asserts that sufficient proof of the Resurrection ought to be found in a passage of Moses where the Resurrection, or Immortality, is not mentioned. The Sadducees, we are told, were put to silence by it.[2] They had no answer ready which was at once plausible and popular, and perhaps the novelty of Christ's argument confounded them. But they were not convinced; and we may imagine one of them saying to another on their way home: "See to what straits the defenders of the doctrine of a Resurrection are driven, when they come to argue the question on the only sure ground of the letter of Scripture! A Pharisee would not have put himself so evidently in the wrong as this poor ignorant Nazarene has done, by quoting as decisive of the question a passage which has no bearing on it whatever." And we may fancy the other replying: "He does not know what a syllogism is. But if he had the faintest idea of logic, he would have seen that his argument tells the opposite way. Because God called Himself the God of Abraham, of Isaac, and of Jacob, after they had lain for centuries dead, it follows that God *is* a God of the dead as well as of the living."

Now, if we confine ourselves to the ground of merely grammatical and logical interpretation, we

[1] 1 Cor. xv. 37-44.   [2] Matt. xxii. 34.

cannot show that the Sadducees would have been wrong in making such comments; and the difficulty would probably be felt more generally than it is, were it not for the prevalence of an almost mechanical conception of Christ's authority. To the believer, the authority of Christ is supreme when He puts it forth. When He says, "*I say unto you, Love your enemies,*"[1] it is the believer's duty to do his best to obey, trusting that by thus doing God's will he will learn to understand the doctrine,[2] and to see its reasonableness, if he does not see it already; and experience shows that he *will* learn to understand it and to see its reasonableness. But this is inapplicable to the passage before us. Christ is not here putting forth His authority; on the contrary, He condescends to reason with His opponents. He does not now preface His words with "I say unto you." He who, in conversation with His trusting friend Martha of Bethany, claimed to be the Resurrection and the Life,[3] here tells the unbelieving and hostile Sadducees that they greatly erred when they failed to read the doctrine of the Resurrection into a passage in Moses where it is not expressly revealed. Now if we, who believe in Christ, are content to accept this argument as a sound one on Christ's mere authority, we shall learn no lesson from it whatever; it will be to us only one among many assertions of the Resurrection, and will certainly not convince any one who remains unconvinced by Saint Paul. What we are meant to

---

[1] Matt. v. 44.   [2] John vii. 17.   [3] John xi. 25.

learn by this passage—so remarkably repeated in the three Synoptic Gospels—is the lawfulness and the duty of interpreting Scripture by the spirit rather than the letter, and bringing higher principles to the work than those of technical grammar and formal logic.

This is a lesson which the Church has not yet sufficiently learned. Worship of the letter is deeply rooted in human nature. Every teacher of those subjects which make demands on the understanding rather than the memory, must, if he knows his business, feel that he has constantly to struggle against the tendency in his pupils to trust to a rule which can be remembered, rather than to a principle which can be understood. In such subjects as logic and mathematics, every one sees that this is a human weakness: a man is not a mathematician, though he may be a calculator, merely because he can apply rules without understanding why they are true; but in religion and theology many make a boast of not ascending from rules to principles. To use expressions which have obtained currency, they demand "chapter and verse for everything," and pride themselves on not going "beyond the things which are written."

As this last expression occurs in Scripture, and, like many other expressions of Scripture, is habitually misapplied, let us examine it in its context. It occurs in that introductory part of the First Epistle to the Corinthians where its author is warning his converts against the spirit of pride, boastfulness, and schism. The entire passage is as follows:—

"Now these things, brethren, I have in a figure transferred to myself and Apollos for your sakes; that in us ye might learn *not to go beyond the things which are written*; that no one of you be puffed up for the one against the other. For who maketh thee to differ? and what hast thou that thou didst not receive? but if thou didst receive it, why dost thou glory, as if thou hadst not received it?"[1]

The translation does not show, what is obvious in the Greek, that the expression "not beyond the things which are written" is quoted as being proverbial. This is implied in the use of the article introducing the quoted clause. The Greek is ἵνα ἐν ἡμῖν μάθητε τὸ μὴ ὑπὲρ ἃ γέγραπται,[2] which Canon Evans[3] translates, or paraphrases, "That you may learn the (lesson), not above what is written," adding, "This expression refers apparently to the moral tenor of the books of the Old Testament. No allusion to a special text.[4] It seems to denote a sort of ethical canon of the Scriptures, and the Corinthian brethren are here exhorted not to transgress this canon, but to keep within its limits by following the specific pattern of modesty and humility adum-

---

[1] 1 Cor. iv. 6, 7.

[2] ἃ (plural) not ὅ (singular) is the reading adopted by the Revisers.

[3] *Speaker's Commentary on the New Testament*, vol. iii. p. 270.

[4] Perhaps there is an allusion to Deut. xvii. 19, 20, a passage written for the guidance of kings. Saint Paul, in the verse following those quoted, says ironically, "Ye have reigned (as kings) without us."

brated to them by Paul and Apollos. This view is strengthened by the moral drift of the citations already made from the Old Testament in this Epistle." Dean Stanley, similarly, paraphrases it by "Learn *that well-known lesson*, not to go beyond what the Scriptures prescribe." If any particular passages of Scripture are alluded to, they are most probably those quoted previously in the same Epistle, all of which tend to inculcate the virtue of humility. They are as follows, quoting not the Old Testament originals, but the Apostle's quotations of them, with his introductory words:—

"The word of the cross is to them that are perishing foolishness; but to us which are being saved it is the power of God. For it is written,

> I will destroy the wisdom of the wise,
> And the prudence of the prudent will I reject."[1]

"Christ Jesus was made unto us wisdom from God, and righteousness, and sanctification, and redemption: that, according as it is written, He that glorieth, let him glory in the Lord."[2]

"The wisdom of this world is foolishness with God. For it is written, He that taketh the wise in their own craftiness.[3] And again, The Lord knoweth the reasonings of the wise, that they are vain."[4]

The proverbial warning, "Not beyond the things

---

[1] Isaiah xxix. 14; 1 Cor. i. 18, 19.
[2] Jer. ix. 24; 1 Cor. i. 30, 31.
[3] Job v. 13; 1 Cor. iii. 19.
[4] Psalm xciv. 11; 1 Cor. iii. 20.

which are written," then, has nothing to do with principles of interpretation, but is directed, with the whole of the first four chapters of this Epistle, against the temper of self-sufficiency, boastfulness, and strife.

If read according to the mere letter, the saying that God is the God of the ancient patriarchs, proves that God is a God of the dead, because the patriarchs have died. But the spirit giveth life, and the spiritual mind has the power and the right to read, between the lines of the Old Testament, the truth that the Divine perfection makes it impossible for God to lose His own elect, or to abandon them in death; that He must therefore be the God of the living, and that the patriarchs, though dead, must be heirs of life. Our Lord, in His comment on this passage, has taught us that in the interpretation of Scripture we *ought* to go beyond the things which are written—beyond the letter to the spirit.

Let us now see how He applies this principle to the actual problems of life.

He more than once calmed a storm on the Lake of Galilee. On the first of these occasions the disciples who were with Him in the boat were much alarmed when the storm came on suddenly; but Christ, when they called on Him, made a "great calm," and then said, "Why are ye so fearful? have ye not yet faith?"[1] implying that they ought to have faith enough to know that He would not only be Himself

[1] Mark iv. 37-40.

preserved through such a danger, but would keep His disciples safe also. He desired to find a faith strong enough to anticipate express revelation.

And this was the faith which He praised when He found it. Ten men who were afflicted with leprosy once saw Him, and cried out, "Jesus, Master, have mercy upon us"; and He, without waiting to touch them, as He usually did in healing, said "Go, show yourselves to the priests" (as commanded by Moses in the case of a cure of leprosy). They went on their way to obey this command, and as they went they saw and felt that the disease had departed. One of them, a Samaritan, then turned back, gave praise to God, and fell down at the feet of Jesus to give Him thanks. The remaining nine obeyed the letter of Christ's command, and went on; the Samaritan disobeyed it in the letter, or at least did what Jesus had not commanded, and he received these words of approval and praise: "Were not the ten cleansed? but where are the nine? Were there none found that returned to give glory to God, save this alien? Arise and go thy way: thy faith hath saved thee."[1]

Similarly, in the case of the Syrophenician, or Canaanite, woman, whose daughter the Lord delivered from the demon which oppressed her, the faith which He approved was a faith which showed itself in trusting in His goodness and mercy against His own words.[2] He answered her first

---

[1] Luke xvii. 12-19.
[2] Matt. xv. 22-28; Mark vii. 25-30.

request for healing with what seemed a refusal: "I am sent only to the lost sheep of the house of Israel"; and when she urged her prayer further, she received what appeared a still harsher refusal: "Let the children first be filled: for it is not meet to take the children's bread, and cast it to the little dogs."[1] But she replied, "Lord, even the little dogs eat of the crumbs which fall from their masters' table." Then at last the Lord answered, saying, "O woman, great is thy faith: be it done unto thee even as thou wilt"; and when she went home she found her daughter quietly lying on her bed and restored to sanity.

The same is taught by the case of the woman suffering from an issue of blood.[2] Her only idea, so far as appears, was that Jesus was so holy a man as to confer power on the very border of the garment which He wore, to heal the most hopeless disease, even without His knowledge. She naturally shrank from publicity, and, watching her opportunity, endeavoured to steal a cure; but Jesus compelled her to make confession, and then said, "Daughter, thy faith hath made thee whole; go in peace, and be whole of thy plague." Although this woman's

---

[1] τοῖς κυναρίοις. Both the Authorised and the Revised Versions have *to the dogs*; but the woman's reply shows that household pets are meant, and the use of the diminutive changes the moral tone of the expression. See Dean Chadwick's *Commentary on St. Mark*, 2nd edition, p. 198 (Hodder and Stoughton).

[2] Mark v. 25-34. See Dean Chadwick (p. 154 *et seq.*) on this subject also.

faith was unspiritual and ignorant, yet Christ approved its simplicity and its strength.

But by far the most remarkable instance of faith outrunning its commission, and receiving Christ's approval, is that of the return of the Seventy.[1] Late in His earthly career, He sent forth seventy of His disciples "into every city and place whither He Himself was about to come"; and said to them in His charge, "Into whatsoever city ye enter, and they receive you . . . heal the sick that are therein." He did not expressly confer any other miraculous power. They knew, however, that, some time before, He had sent forth the Twelve on a similar mission, but with express authority not only to heal the sick, but to cast out demons:[2] the Seventy tried to do the same, and succeeded. They "returned with joy, saying, Lord, even the demons are subject unto us through Thy name." And Jesus "said unto them, I beheld Satan fallen as lightning from heaven. Behold, I have given you authority to tread upon serpents and scorpions, and over all the power of the enemy"; which words may be thus paraphrased—"Your victories over the power of evil are Mine and My Father's; and I place all My earthly power at your disposal, for the accomplishment of the work that I have given you to do." Theirs was the victory of faith. Compare, by way of contrast, the sons of Sceva.[3] They, like Simon the sorcerer,[4] thought the

[1] Luke x. [2] Luke ix.
[3] Acts xix. 13 et seq. [4] Acts viii. 9 et seq.

miraculous powers of the Apostles of Christ were only a more potent kind of magic than their own: they tried to use the name of Jesus against the demons, but found it powerless on their lips.

From all this teaching of Our Lord, we learn that the faith which He approves is not a faith which "demands chapter and verse for everything," and carefully examines the records of Revelation with a microscope of interpretation, in fear of unawares exaggerating the riches of the promises of God. The faith which He approves is in the spirit, not in the letter: it is a faith which can anticipate the unfolding of God's purposes, and knows how to read between the lines of revelation.[1] Love hopeth all things.[2]

[1] I quote the following from "Faith and Sight," a sermon by the Rev. Hamilton Stewart Verschoyle, in the *Church of England Pulpit*, 26th Sept. 1891.

"Sometimes when thoughts of the omnipotence of God's Righteousness and Love, and their assurance of their ultimate victory in leading all from sin to righteousness, are brought forward, people say, 'I would believe this if you could show me texts to prove it, or if you could point it out to me in the authoritative teaching of the Church.' I believe many texts can be produced in reply to such a demand, to say nothing of the drift of Scripture teaching as to the character of God; but is not the demand itself, as requiring such evidence as a condition precedent to faith, a seeking to walk by sight and not by faith? Can we not believe in the omnipotence—I speak, of course, of a moral omnipotence—of Our Father's righteousness and love, unless we see it down in black and white—unless we have the evidence of sight for it? Must not the highest ideal be nearer truth than a lower one?"

[2] 1 Cor. xiii. 7.

Thus, when we are told, on the strength of the apparent grammatical meaning of passages of Scripture, or of logical inference from them, that there is no hope for those who depart out of the present life unreconciled to God, we have a right to say *The Lord* Jehovah, the Eternal, *will not always chide: neither will He keep His anger for ever.*[1] Christ is the Prince of Peace;[2] God is the God of Hope,[3] and His name is Love.[4] The Prince of Peace cannot for ever be at war with those over whom He reigns; the God of Hope cannot leave any in hopelessness; and the God who is Love will sooner or later be reconciled to all. When we are told that we shall lose for eternity any of those whom we have loved on earth, we have a right to reply, *He that spared not His own Son, but delivered Him up for us all, shall He not also with Him freely give us all things?*[5] *We are more than conquerors through Him that loved us*[6]—conquerors not only for ourselves, but for others. *God is able to do exceeding abundantly above all that we can ask or think;*[7] and why should He remind us of this, unless He were not only able but willing? *Whether the world, or life, or death, or things present, or things to come; all are* ours; *and we are Christ's; and Christ is God's.*[8] When we are told that the possibilities of God's mercy are bounded by place and time—by the limits of this world and of the present life—we have a right

---

[1] Psalm ciii. 9. [2] Isaiah ix. 6. [3] Romans xv. 13.
[4] 1st Epistle of John iv. 8, 16. [5] Romans viii. 32.
[6] Romans viii. 37. [7] Eph. iii. 20. [8] 1 Cor. iii. 22.

to say, *Jesus Christ is the same yesterday, to-day, yea and for ever.*[1] When we are told that His mercy is for those only who are the favoured of His own arbitrary election, we have a right to say, *The Lord is good to all: and His tender mercies are over all His works. The Lord upholdeth all that fall, and raiseth all that be bowed down.*[2] When we are told that the death of the body is a barrier which the mercy of God through Christ is unable to overpass, we have a right to say that Christ, while on earth—"a power girt round with weakness"—was able to raise the dead to life; and now that He is enthroned "at the right hand of the Majesty on high,"[3] as "Lord of both the dead and the living,"[4] and endowed with all authority in heaven and earth,[5] it is impossible that His power to save can stop short at the gate of death. It is not the will of our Father in Heaven—so Christ has said—that one of the little ones should perish.[6] Every human being either is, or has been, a little child; and it is not possible that the will of God can be for ever defeated. When we are reminded of Christ's declaration that many indeed are called but few chosen,[7] we have a right to reply that although this is obviously true of the present world, yet He has suggested a very different hope of the ultimate fate of mankind in the parable of the one sheep that strays away while the ninety and nine

---

[1] Hebrews xiii. 8.   [2] Psalm cxlv. 9, 14.
[3] Hebrews i. 3.   [4] Romans xiv. 9.   [5] Matt. xxviii. 18.
[6] Matt. xviii. 14.   [7] Matt. xxii. 14.

remain in safety.[1] A parable asserts nothing; but the suggestion of this parable is, that as God's power is not limited by space nor His knowledge by time, so His mercy and His love are not limited by number; and that He cares for each one of His intelligent creatures as if it were the only one in the universe. And when we are told that for a large part—perhaps the majority—of mankind, it would have been better not to have been born, we have a right to say that *the yoke of Christ is easy and His burden is light*,[2] and He cannot require His people to bear the overwhelming and crushing burden of such a belief.

Such sayings as these are as decisive of the infinity and universality of the grace of God, as is the declaration "I am the God of Abraham" of the truth of immortality: these are ground enough for eternal hope, even without the more definite declarations on which we have dwelt in a previous chapter. But besides declarations of this kind, Our Lord's appeal remains—"Why even of yourselves judge ye not what is right?"[3] declaring that the revelation of God is not meant to supersede, but to evoke, the naturally-given power of discerning truth from falsehood and good from evil. And certainly it is worthy of the Divine character, that we should trust God to be not less but more gracious than even His own words—to fulfil all, and more than all, the hopes which His most gracious words excite. It is only from human goodness that we can form any

---

[1] Matt. xviii. 12.   [2] Matt. xi. 30.   [3] Luke xii. 57.

conception of Divine goodness; and he is not the best man or the most like to God, of whom it can be said that he may be trusted to keep his promise to the letter, but that no importance must be attached to any expression or suggestion of his goodwill which does not amount to a promise.

In conclusion;—Supposing the conception of the Divine character and purposes set forth in this and the previous chapters to be true; supposing God to be both perfectly just and infinitely gracious, having a Fatherly purpose of final good to all, and permitting the existence of sin and suffering only for a time, and only for the sake of the higher good to be evolved through the struggle against them; supposing further that there is a necessity, in the uncreated nature of things, for justice to be vindicated before grace can have free course, and that the purpose of grace can be attained only through justice; and supposing that God designs to further the salvation of men by revealing to them His character and His purposes, insofar as it is possible for men to learn and good for men to know;—Supposing these doctrines to be true, to what extent, and in what form, might we reasonably expect the ultimate purposes of God towards mankind to be revealed?

We ought to expect that the greatest and most evident stress should be laid on those parts of religion which are the least acceptable to the natural mind of man, and yet constitute the foundation of the entire system; namely, the absolute duty of obedience to the moral law and the commandments of God, the "sinfulness of sin," the sacredness of justice, and the certainty of judgment. And, forasmuch as it is useless to hold up to men an evidently unapproachable ideal, we might expect that from the first there should be hints and suggestions of salvation — promises from God that He will take the part of good against evil, not only in a future judgment, but in the present strife. We should also expect that revelation should be progressive, so that the Law of Justice should be earlier made known than the Gospel of Grace. Further, it would not appear strange if the formation of an elect Church, to receive blessing itself from the first and to be the channel of ultimate blessing to the rest of mankind, should be a conspicuous part of the Providential plan. After the revelation of justice, we might expect a revelation of mercy; and after the formation of an elect Church, the revelation that the fact of election is temporary and provisional, and destined to merge and end in the conferring of Divine favour on all. But we should expect the utmost prominence to be given to the manifestation of the righteousness of God in judgment, and the total overthrow of whatever is opposed to His righteous will: while all beyond this— any more decisive purpose of final and universal mercy and grace than that which we now see at work—should be revealed, not clearly, but only in doubtful hints and suggestions.

Of course I do not mean that any man, without the Prophetic Spirit of God, could have thought out all this for himself. But when it has been revealed, we can see that it is consistent with the highest ideas which we can form of God. Now, this is what we actually find; this is what is actually revealed: except only, that the revelation of final mercy to all is very much clearer and more definite than we could have dared to hope.[1] As the privileges of the elect race of Abraham have been merged in those of the elect Church of Christ, so shall these, in their turn, be merged in the ultimate salvation of all.

[1] See especially the quotations from the New Testament in the chapter on the Final Destiny of the Rejected.

NOTE TO CHAPTER VIII.

SAINT IGNATIUS ON THE LETTER AND THE SPIRIT.

The following, from one of the Epistles of Ignatius to the Philadelphians, as quoted from Lightfoot's *Apostolic Fathers* in Bishop Alexander's *Leading Ideas of the Gospels*, p. 21, clearly asserts the right of the believer in Christ to go beyond the mere letter, and to read between the lines of Holy Scripture. The translation which I offer is somewhat closer to the Greek than Bishop Alexander's.

ἐπεὶ ἤκουσά τινων λεγόντων ὅτι Ἐὰν μὴ ἐν τοῖς ἀρχείοις εὕρω ἐν τῷ εὐαγγελίῳ οὐ πιστεύω, καὶ λέγοντός μου αὐτοῖς ὅτι Γέγραπται· ἀπεκρίθησάν μοι ὅτι Πρόκειται· ἐμοὶ δὲ ἀρχεῖά ἐστιν Ἰησοῦς Χριστός, τὰ ἄθικτα ἀρχεῖα ὁ σταυρὸς αὐτοῦ καὶ ὁ θάνατος καὶ ἡ ἀνάστασις αὐτοῦ καὶ ἡ πίστις ἡ δι᾽ αὐτῶν.

"When I have heard some say, Unless I find this in the archives, I do not believe it is in the Gospel: and I said to them, It is written: they answered me, That is the question. But for me the archives are Jesus Christ—the inviolable archives are His cross and His death and His resurrection, and the faith which is through them."

CHAPTER IX.

SAINT PAUL ON PREDESTINATION.

[The present chapter is reproduced, with some alterations and omissions, from an article of the writer's, bearing the same title, in the *Expositor*, second series, vol. vii., 1884.]

THE subject of God's judgment and man's responsibility naturally raises the question of man's freedom, and the relation of that freedom to God's absolute Foreknowledge and omnipotent Will. In the present chapter, I propose to consider the teaching of those very few passages of Holy Scripture which touch on this question.

The word "foreordain" is substituted in the Revised Version for "predestinate," in Romans viii. 29; "to ordain" being a common word in Biblical English, while "to destine" and "destiny" do not occur there. I follow their example by substituting "foreordain" and "foreordination" for "predestinate" and "predestination."

The Epistle to the Philippians is perhaps on the whole the most interesting of the writings of Saint

Paul. It has all the theological depth of the Epistles to the Romans and to the Ephesians, and its interest arising out of personal friendship is as strong as that of the Epistles to the Thessalonians or of the Pastoral Epistles.

In this Epistle we read the following words:—
"So then, my beloved, even as ye have always obeyed, not as in my presence only, but now much more in my absence, work out your own salvation with fear and trembling; for it is God which worketh in you both to will and to work, for His good pleasure."[1] This passage has been claimed as supporting their different views, by both Calvinists and Arminians; that is to say, those who maintain the doctrine of election and foreordination in the most rigid sense, and those who maintain some independent efficiency in the will of man; and it has been said, sarcastically but truly, that the opposite treatment of the passage by those two schools consists merely in this, that the Arminian reads it, "*Work out your own salvation* with fear and trembling; for it is God that worketh in you both to will and to work, for His good pleasure"; while the Calvinist reads it, "Work out your own salvation with fear and trembling; for *it is God that worketh in you both to will and to work, for His good pleasure.*"[2]

It is, however, doing injustice to this passage to

[1] Philippians ii. 12, 13.
[2] The chief emphasis in this passage, however, is not really on the antithesis between "your work" and "God's work in

bring it into controversy at all. There is a real difficulty in the question concerning the relation between the will of God and that of man; but the passage before us, though by its mode of expression it suggests the difficulty, has no bearing whatever on the solution. Its purpose is purely practical. It follows one of the strongest assertions to be found in Holy Scripture of Christ's former humiliation and present glory; and it is followed by an exhortation to purity in the midst of an evil world. The problem of the relation between the will of God and that of man was not before the Apostle's mind when he wrote it; and the apparent contradiction—speaking in the first clause as if God's will were everything, and in the second as if man's will were everything—is due to Saint Paul's condensed and elliptical style, which leaves the reader to seize for himself the connection of the thoughts.

But how is it possible for the will of God to

you," but on that between Paul's absence from his Philippian converts and God's presence in them. I quote from Lightfoot *in loco*:—"Having the example of Christ's humiliation to guide you, and the example of Christ's exaltation to encourage you, as ye have always been obedient hitherto, so continue. Do not look to my encouragement to stimulate you. Labour earnestly not only at times when I am with you, but now when I am far away. With a nervous and trembling anxiety work out your salvation for yourselves. For yourselves, did I say? Nay, ye are not alone; it is God which worketh in you." Compare the words of the second Collect at evening prayer: "O God, from whom all holy desires, all good counsels, and all just works do proceed."

work through the will of man without superseding and annulling it? This is a mystery which man's understanding is not altogether competent to solve; but its solution is in no way necessary to faith in God; just as the somewhat similar, though lower, mysteries of the relation between the vital and the chemical forces in the processes of nutrition and organisation, and between the mental forces and the unconscious functions of the nervous system — in other words, the relations between matter and life, and between unconscious life and mind — must be recognised as insoluble, without therefore giving up all research into the laws of life and of mind.

Controversialists on both sides will probably agree that the question may be thus formulised: Does God's foreordination depend on His foreknowledge, or His foreknowledge on His foreordination? Now, before inquiring what Saint Paul says on this subject, let us ask the previous question, whether this difficulty ever presented itself to the Apostle's mind as one that needed a definite solution. I think it can be shown that it did not. The question in his time was not felt as a practical one. Israelites who were rejoicing that the promised Messiah had come, and Gentiles who knew that they had been saved by the Gospel of Christ from "abominable idolatries," were not likely to distress themselves and show distrust of their Saviour by asking, "How can I be certain of my own individual foreordination to eternal life?" But if this question, which has perplexed so many minds since the period of the Reformation, had been asked of Saint Paul, we can see plainly enough, from his writings, how he would have answered it. Most of his epistles are addressed to congregations, and he always addresses these as consisting of men whom God had called and chosen. We consequently cannot doubt that his reply would have been somewhat to this effect: "The fact that you confess Christ and seek salvation, is proof enough that you are of God's elect. God is your Father, and as a Father pitieth his children, so the Lord pitieth them that fear Him.[1] You are already in possession of all Christian privileges, and we have a right to be confident that He who has begun a good work in you will perfect it until the day of Jesus Christ.[2] But these privileges may be lost by abusing or neglecting them; wherefore, let him who thinketh he standeth take heed lest he fall."[3]

It is in this, and not in any absolute sense, that Saint Paul habitually speaks of election.[4] Probably the most signal instance of the kind is in his first epistle to his Thessalonian converts: "Knowing, brethren beloved of God, your election; how that our Gospel came not unto you in word only, but also in power, and in the Holy Spirit, and in much

---

[1] Psalm ciii. 13.   [2] Philippians i. 6.   [3] 1 Cor. x. 12.
[4] See the chapter on Election in Archbishop Whately's *Difficulties of Saint Paul*. It is somewhat remarkable, however, that Whately does not mention the passage, Romans viii. 28, 30, which most persons probably regard, though I do not, as the "classical passage" on election. See farther on.

assurance."[1] Although Saint Paul had heard the voice of Jesus Christ after His ascension, and had been caught up into the third heaven,[2] he did not pretend to know more than the newest of his converts about the secret purposes of God: it was not a matter of revelation to him that the Christians of Thessalonica were elect to final glory in God's inscrutable counsel "before eternal times"; and it is not possible that during his sojourn in Thessalonica he could have acquired so intimate an acquaintance with every member of the Church as to be able to say that he was morally certain of the final perseverance unto salvation of them all.

In one well-known passage, however, he departs from his customary use of words, and speaks of a calling not to Christian privileges only, but to eternal glory. "To them that love God, all things work together for good, even to them that are called according to His purpose. For whom He foreknew, He also foreordained to be conformed to the image of His Son, that He might be the firstborn among many brethren; and whom He foreordained, them He also called; and whom He called, them He also justified; and whom He justified, them He also glorified. What then shall we say to these things? If God is for us, who is against us? . . . Who shall lay anything to the charge of God's elect? It is God that justifieth; who is he that shall condemn?"[3]

---

[1] 1 Thess. i. 4, 5.   [2] 2 Cor. xii. 2 *et seq.*
[3] Rom. viii. 28-34.

It is further to be remarked, that Saint Paul's language concerning the relation of the will of man to the will of God is uncertain, and might be called wavering by those who demand a certain utterance on all controverted questions. In one place he says: "Who maketh thee to differ? and what hast thou that thou didst not receive? But if thou didst receive it, why dost thou glory as if thou hadst not received it?"[1] This passage, taken alone, would appear to show that he regarded the Divine will as everything, and the human will as nothing. But in the passage from the Epistle to the Romans which we have been considering, the words "whom God foreknew, He also foreordained," appear to show that Saint Paul regarded foreordination, or election, as depending on foreknowledge; and it is perhaps significant that this expression occurs in a passage where the Apostle speaks of "calling" and foreordination in a somewhat higher than the usual sense. In the passage from the Epistle to the Philippians with which we began our examination of the subject, we have noticed that he does not show himself conscious of the existence of any such question. The only possible inference from the comparison of these three passages—one of them seemingly on each side of the question, and the third neutral—is that on this subject Saint Paul did not think it needful to have any formulated opinion.

[1] 1 Cor. iv. 7.

I shall now endeavour to show that the same conclusion is warranted by the passage in the Epistle to the Romans (ix. 6 *et seq.*), which has been so often quoted in favour of the most rigid doctrine of Divine election. It is the only passage where Saint Paul shows any consciousness of moral or metaphysical difficulty arising out of the question of foreordination. It is a digression in the middle of a chapter which begins with a lamentation over the rejection of the Christ by the mass of the people of Israel. He justifies the action of God in permitting this, by recalling that the promises of God to the children of Abraham were not to all the children, but only to the chosen ones;—to Isaac and not to Ishmael; to Jacob and not to Esau. And this election, to use a human mode of speech, is purely arbitrary. "The children being not yet born, neither having done anything good or bad, that the purpose of God according to election might stand, not of works, but of Him that calleth; it was said, The elder shall serve the younger.[1] Even as it is written, Jacob I loved, but Esau I hated."[2] It would be impossible to assert more distinctly the unconditionalness of God's election. But to what were these two brothers respectively elected? There is nothing here about election to any position, good or bad, in the eternal world. Jacob was loved by God, and was elected to be a "prince of God" and an ancestor of David and of Christ.

[1] Gen. xxv. 23. [2] Mal. i. 2, 3.

Esau was loved less; this is all that "hated" can mean here; for, in the usual sense of the word, hatred seeks to destroy; and so far was God from destroying Esau, that he was permitted to receive a blessing, though an inferior blessing to that of Jacob, and to become the father of a nation. The elder served the younger; but service, even the lowest, is not reprobation, and is scarcely compatible with it.

In this case there is no moral difficulty whatever. But the same cannot be said of the instance of Pharaoh, which the Apostle mentions immediately after. I quote the entire passage (Epistle to the Romans ix. 17-24), inserting comments of my own, which are marked [thus]:—

"The Scripture saith unto Pharaoh, For this very purpose did I raise thee up, that I might show in thee My power, and that My name might be published abroad in all the earth. So then He hath mercy on whom He will, and whom He will He hardeneth." [In Biblical language hardness of heart does not mean cruelty, but judicial blindness; and to say that God hardened Pharaoh's heart, means that he was abandoned to his own pride and obstinacy; just as the men of the Gentile world generally, according to Saint Paul in the same Epistle, were given over to a reprobate mind as a punishment for refusing to have God in their knowledge.[1] In the ordinary Divine government, the neglect of the

[1] Rom. i. 28.

means of grace is punished by their withdrawal—a truth which all systems of religious philosophy alike must accept as part of their data.] "Thou wilt then say unto me, Why doth He yet find fault? for who withstandeth His will?" [That is to say, Does not God's sovereignty, then, supersede and annul man's responsibility? If men's actions are foreordained, how can any man be judged guilty?] "Nay but, O man, who art thou that repliest against God? Shall the thing formed say to Him that formed it, Why didst thou make me thus? Or hath not the potter a right over the clay, from the same lump to make one part a vessel unto honour, and another unto dishonour? What if God, willing to show His wrath, and to make His power known" [an allusion to v. 17: "For this very purpose did I raise thee up, that I might show in thee My power"], "endured with much longsuffering vessels of wrath fitted to destruction" [fitted by what agency? This question is not answered, nor asked, here: but there can be no doubt the Apostle believed that they are fitted to destruction, not by God's will, but through their own fault. He does not say that God *makes* them so, but that God *endures* them. Compare 1 Timothy ii. 4: "God our Saviour, who willeth that all men should be saved and come to a knowledge of the truth"]; "and that He might make known the riches of His glory upon vessels of mercy, which He afore prepared unto glory, even us?"

The illustration of the absolute sovereignty of God from the right of the potter over the clay is an allusion to Isaiah lxiv. 8, and Jeremiah xviii. 1-6. But does Saint Paul mean this as a full account of the matter? Does he really mean that the relation of God to His creatures whom He has endowed with capacity to know and to love Him, is fitly and fully symbolised by that of a potter to his vessels? I well remember being repelled, during early life, from the study of Saint Paul's writings by the belief that such was his doctrine. But the rest of his works contain ample proof that he did not regard this as the final word on the subject; and the passage before us, alone, is sufficient to show that he does not regard this illustration as exhausting the question. The inconsistency of the metaphorical language shows his consciousness that the illustration is incomplete.

Has not the Divine Potter a right over the clay of human nature, of the same lump to make one vessel for an honourable and another for a dishonourable use, but each for its own use? Moses was a vessel of honour; he honoured God, and was honoured by God. Pharaoh was a vessel of dishonour; he is remembered for his cruelty, pride, and infatuation. But God had his own use for each. Moses willingly and gladly served God, by leading Israel out of Egypt and founding the Israelite nation. Pharaoh also, but unwillingly and blindly, served God by expelling Israel from Egypt; for if the Israelites had been treated by their masters with kindness, they would most probably have been merged and lost in the Egyptian people, and there would have been no Israelite nation.

> Blindly the wicked work
> The righteous will of Heaven.[1]

But though the Divine Potter makes at His own pleasure vessels of honour and vessels of dishonour, there is no suggestion here, or anywhere else in Saint Paul's writings, that He makes vessels for the purpose of being

> destroyed,
> Or cast as rubbish to the void.[2]

The forming of vessels for different and opposite uses is, as we have seen, directly referred by Saint Paul to the sovereign will of God; but this does not answer, nor even touch, the further question concerning vessels which, so far as man can see, are nothing but vessels of wrath, fitted only to destruction. On this subject Saint Paul has absolutely nothing to suggest; he only speaks of the long-suffering of God; but where he speaks of vessels of wrath, he avoids mentioning the Potter. Whether conscious or not—and I believe it is perfectly conscious—this failure to carry the metaphor consistently through the passage is a confession that he cannot give a full account of the matter; that the difficulty cannot be fully solved.

It is worth remark here, how the word repro-

---

[1] Southey's *Thalaba*.   [2] *In Memoriam*.

bation, which, by its etymology, and in the language of Scripture, means rejection as the result of trial, like a gun that does not stand the proof charge, came in Calvinistic theology to mean rejection by arbitrary decree, independently of trial. This violent change in the meaning of a common and perfectly intelligible word, is a strong presumption against the truth of the theory under the influence of which the change was made.

NOTE TO CHAPTER IX.

The following is from *Sonnets and other Poems, chiefly religious,* by the present writer.

THE POTTER AND THE CLAY.

WHY hast Thou made me so,
My Maker? I would know
Wherefore Thou gav'st me such a mournful dower:
Toil that is oft in vain,
Knowledge that deepens pain,
And longing to be pure, without the power?

"Shall the thing formed aspire
The purpose to require
Of Him who formed it?" Make not answer thus!
Beyond the Potter's wheel
There lieth an appeal
To Him who breathed the breath of life in us.

"The Potter and the Clay."

> When the same power that made
>   My being, has arrayed
> Its nature with a dower of sin and woe,
>   And thoughts that question all :
>   Why should the words appal
> That ask the Maker why He made it so ?
>
> I know we are but clay,
>   Thus moulded to display
> His wisdom and His power who rolls the years ;—
>   Whose wheel is Heaven and earth—
>   Its motion, death and birth ;—
> Is Potter, then, the name that most endears ?
>
> To Him we bow as King :
>   As Lord His praise we sing :
> We pray to Him as Father and as God :
>   Saviour in our distress,
>   Guide through the wilderness,
> And Judge that beareth an avenging rod.
>
> I grudge not, Lord, to be
>   Of meanest use to Thee ;—
> Make me a trough for swine, if so Thou wilt ;—
>   But if my vessel's clay
>   Be marred and thrown away
> Before it takes its form, is mine the guilt ?
>
> I trust Thee to the end,
>   Creator, Saviour, Friend,
> Whatever name Thou deignest that we call.
>   Art Thou not good and just ?
>   I wait and watch, and trust
> That Love is still Thy holiest name of all.
>
> I watch and strive all night ;
>   And when the morning's light
> Shines on the path I travelled here below ;
>   When day eternal breaks,
>   And life immortal wakes,
> Then shalt Thou tell me why Thou mad'st me so.

CHAPTER X.

A PHYSICAL THEORY OF MORAL FREEDOM.

[The present chapter is an expansion of a paper with the same title, contributed by the writer to the proceedings of the Victoria Institute.]

IN the foregoing chapter, we have considered the question of the relation of the human Will to the Divine Power and Foreknowledge, as seen in the light thrown on it by the greatest of the Apostles of Christ. We have now to consider the same human Will in its relation to the laws of matter and of purely mechanical force.

John Stuart Mill has quoted from some unnamed writer—perhaps himself—that "on all great subjects much remains to be said." It is, however, likely that he would have made an exception of those subjects which are contemptuously called metaphysical by that Positivist school whereof he was in his time the ablest English exponent; perhaps he would have said that they are partly solved and partly proved to be insoluble, and that on this question of Freedom and

Necessity the last word which has been, or can be, spoken, is, not that Freedom is proved impossible—Mill was too cautious a reasoner to commit himself to such an assertion—but that no valid reason can be given for thinking Freedom possible, and thereby admitting that there can be any exception or limitation to the absolute uniformity of the order of Nature; including in this order not only unconscious Nature, but conscious Mind. And this appears to be the general belief of that philosophical, or scientific, school, which is dominant among us, and has Herbert Spencer as its chief living exponent. Some, indeed, speak as if they thought this absolute uniformity of the course of things was of the nature of a logical truth, which cannot be denied without affirming a contradiction. But the more general and plausible opinion is that this uniformity follows by mathematical necessity from the laws of physical nature.

I think, on the contrary, that this question of Freedom and Necessity is not, and probably may never be, a closed question. I think it one of those "great questions on which much remains to be said"; and I propose to give an account of some views on the subject, which have been published by French writers during the last few years.

The question in dispute must first be stated; for I believe there are many who really affirm this doctrine of absolute and unalterable uniformity in the order of things—philosophical Necessity, as it was formerly called, or Determinism, as it is called now—

and yet say that in some transcendental sense they are believers in Moral Freedom. If I do not misunderstand them, this is the position of Dr. Chalmers and of the Duke of Argyll. The question cannot be stated in more suitable words than those of Professor Delbœuf, of Liège [1]:—

"The fundamental proposition of determinism is the following:—The present state of the universe, and consequently the movement of the least of its atoms, is the necessary and only possible consequence of its immediately preceding state, and the sufficient cause of its immediately following state; so that a sufficiently powerful intelligence would be able from a single glance (at the present state of the universe) to infer its entire past and its entire future.

"The partial denial of this proposition will evidently give the definition (of freedom) which we seek:—Freedom is a faculty or power, which produces movements which are not implied (*renfermés*) in the immediately preceding movements, and consequently cannot be predicted" (by any intelligence, however powerful, which acts under the same conditions as ours).

I have added the concluding words to Delbœuf's, because I believe that the Divine Intelligence does not exist under the same conditions as that of Man, but transcends time, and comprehends all things past, present, and future.

---

[1] *Bulletin de l'Académie Royale de Belgique.* 3me serie, tome 1, No. 4, 1881.—3me serie, No. 2, 1882. The quotation in the text is from the latter of these two memoirs.

I do not propose here to go back on the metaphysical aspect of the controversy, but to treat it only in its relations to physical science.

The physical or mechanical, as distinguished from the metaphysical, difficulty in recognising Will as an agency capable of acting on matter was, I believe, first seen by Descartes. He taught that matter and spirit, though in union, are absolutely distinct; that matter acts, and is acted on, according to rigidly mechanical laws; and that the total quantity of motion in the universe is invariable. From these premises it is an obvious consequence that Will cannot be a source of motive power in the universe of matter; but Descartes solved the difficulty by adding that Will, though unable to produce motion, is able to direct it. I believe this to be in substance the true solution; and it is substantially that of at least two of the three writers of whose views I have undertaken to give an account; but it needs to be translated into not only the language, but the ideas of modern science. "Quantity of motion," in this context, is not an accurate expression; but the truth after which Descartes was groping is what is now known as the doctrine of the Conservation of Energy;—that the energy of the universe, though perpetually undergoing transformation, is a constant quantity; that a given quantity of energy, when it undergoes transformation, does an exactly equivalent quantity of work, which work reappears in some other form of energy. Muscular action presents no exception to this law of Conservation; for it is disputed by none, that the energy put forth in muscular action is not created by an effort of the Will, but has previously existed in the animal organism, stored up in some form which can be drawn on when needed for use.

Expressed in modern language, the mechanical argument against the possibility of Freedom is that Freedom would be inconsistent with the law of the Conservation of Energy. Freedom, as Delbœuf has defined it in the passage quoted above, implies that it would have been possible for certain events to have befallen differently from what actually has befallen; and it is asserted that, if this had been the case, the sum total of energy in the universe would have been changed either by increase or by decrease — which is impossible.

One reply to this is, that energy may be transformed, without either gain or loss of quantity, under the influence of a force which remains unchanged, and does not itself pass into energy. Thus, in a "dynamo," or generator of electricity for illuminating or other purposes, the motive energy, due to the fall of water or the expansion of steam, is transformed into electricity, under the influence of magnets which themselves undergo neither increase nor diminution of magnetic power; and it may be argued that the function of the Will, in determining the transformation of nervous and muscular energy, is analogous to that of the magnets of the dynamo; being unable to produce energy in the smallest quantity, but able to direct its transformation in one way rather than in another.[1] This, however, appears a very unsatisfactory analogy. The static force of the magnets belongs to the same order of being with the current of electricity, being related to it somewhat as pressure to motion; while Will is not a physical force, but is of another order of being from matter and its forces.

Another possible reply is, that the Will may determine the time and manner of the transformation of energy, somewhat in the same way that, in mechanism, a very small force is able to guide the action of a very great one. For instance, the steam-engines which propel a large ship, though they work up to several thousand horse-power, can be started or stopped by the hand of the engineer, who moves a lever with the exertion of an amount of muscular force almost infinitesimally smaller than that of the engines which he controls. And it would be possible indefinitely to diminish the muscular power needed, until the gentlest finger-touch on an electric button was sufficient to control the most powerful engines that human art can construct. This is not only theoretically possible, but within the actual resources of our engineers. In the largest steamers, the engineer's hand does not directly work the valves which start, stop, or reverse the engines; those valves are worked

---

[1] This suggestion, though differently expressed, appears to be fundamentally identical with one made on the same subject in an article on Atomic Theories in the *North British Review* of March 1868.

by a steam-engine of very small power in proportion to the engines that propel the ship, which small engine is under the engineer's direct control. And similarly, the rudder is not worked directly by the steersman, but by a small steam-engine which the steersman controls. And to mention a still more striking instance of a very great force controlled by a very small one;—a touch on an electric button by a child of ten years old exploded the vast mines of dynamite which in a moment rent the rocks of Hellgate asunder, and opened a new channel into the harbour of New York for the largest ships in the world. Are not these significant symbols of the control of Will over the muscular forces?

But in reply to this, it is urged that the analogy fails unless it were possible for the will of the engineer to control the engines without the exertion of muscular power at all; and however this may be diminished by refinement of mechanism, it can never be reduced absolutely to nothing.

Sir John Herschel saw the difficulty, and appears to have concluded that the will can and does produce energy, though in quantity so minute as to be incapable of experimental proof. This is cutting the knot rather than untying it. I quote his words: " The actual *force* necessary to be *originated* to give rise to the utmost imaginable exertion of animal power in any case, may be no greater than is required to remove a single material molecule from its place through a space inconceivably minute;—no more in comparison with the dynamical force *disengaged*, directly or indirectly, by the act, than the pull of a hair-trigger in comparison with the force of the mine which it explodes. But without the power to make *some* material disposition, to originate *some* movement, or to change, at least temporarily, the amount of dynamical force appropriate to some one or more material molecules, the mechanical results of human or animal volition are inconceivable. It matters not that we are ignorant of the mode in which this is performed. It suffices to bring the origination of dynamical power, to however small an extent, within the domain of acknowledged personality."[1]

A French writer of our time—Professor Armand Sabatier, of Montpellier—has proposed to cut the knot in another way, by questioning the absolute uniformity of the order of nature.[2] He admits, of course, that all motions on the largest scale, that is to say, those of the celestial bodies, and indeed of all masses which are visible to the unassisted eye, are absolutely determined; but he suggests that this may not be true of those molecular motions which modern science has proved to exist everywhere; and, as he truly remarks, it is not in the greatest but in the minutest actions that the nature of matter is in any degree revealed to us. Light consists of undulations in an ethereal substance, moving, so long as the light

[1] *Familiar Lectures on Scientific Subjects*, p. 468.
[2] In a series of articles entitled *Evolution et Liberté*, in the *Revue Chrétienne* of April, May, September, and October 1885.

is not polarised, in every plane at right angles to the direction of the ray; and the heat of bodies consists of vibrations of their molecules, moving, no doubt, in every direction at once. Sabatier suggests that these motions are in some degree undetermined, and not subject to any rigid law of uniformity; and he finds traces of the same indeterminism in some motions which are on a sufficiently large scale to be visible under the microscope. One instance of this which he mentions is that of the "Brownian" motions of minute particles suspended in water or other liquids.[1] These movements are of very small amplitude, but incessant, of quite sensible rapidity, and in every direction at once. They are well seen in ink, when a drop is placed between two flat pieces of glass; and it is these motions which prevent ink from losing its properties as such, by the subsidence of the black particles.

On this subject it is to be remarked that the laws of motion are perfectly simple; though not mathematical in the nature of their evidence—for they are proved only by experiment, and have not that self-evidencing character which belongs to mathematical truth—yet they are mathematical in form; though the proof that they are absolutely true is never per-

---

[1] So named after the eminent botanist, Robert Brown, who first called attention to their importance. Professor Jevons (*Quarterly Journal of Science*, April 1878) offers what appears to be a satisfactory explanation of these motions, as being due to minute disturbances of electric equilibrium, and analogous to the motions of pith-balls in a well-known electrical experiment.

fectly complete, yet every increase in the accuracy and perfection of astronomical knowledge brings us nearer to such absolute proof; and it seems extremely improbable that they should be subject to any limit whatever. The Brownian motions, the motions of the molecules of gases, the undulatory motion which constitutes light — all these, however minute, are motions, and we cannot doubt that they are rigidly subject to the laws of motion. It is uncertain how far chemical actions can be resolved into the motions of atoms; but the law of the absolute invariability of chemical properties and actions — the proof of which, it is true, can never be complete, though every increase of chemical knowledge strengthens it — makes it probable, with a probability approaching indefinitely near to certainty, that the laws of chemical action admit of no more limitation or exception than the laws of motion. We must consequently hold with scientific men generally, that all motions, whether on a planetary or an atomic scale of magnitude, are determined by the laws of motion, with a certainty which, though not mathematical in its nature, is practically equal to mathematical certainty.

But do the laws of motion ensure absolute determinism? An attempt has been made by Professor Boussinesq, of Lille, to show that absolute determinism, though generally true in mathematics, is not always so, and therefore is not necessarily always true in mechanics.[1] He chiefly makes use in his argument

[1] See Paul Janet's article in the *Contemporary Review*, June 1878.

of what are called singular solutions. We must here state when and how a singular solution arises, for the term is by no means self-explaining.

A set of curves are drawn which we shall call C, C', C", etc. They are not in general mathematically similar, but constitute a family, varying continuously from curve to curve according to a definite law. They are indefinite in number and indefinitely near to each other, and are so drawn that C intersects with C', C' with C", and so on. A curve S, which is generally of a totally distinct kind from the curves C, is so drawn through these intersections that the curves C are tangential to S; making the relation of S to the curves C somewhat like that of a circle to its tangents. S is called the envelope of the curves C, and it is "singular," that is to say unique, and not one of a family like the curves C.

The following diagram shows the relation of the curves C to S:

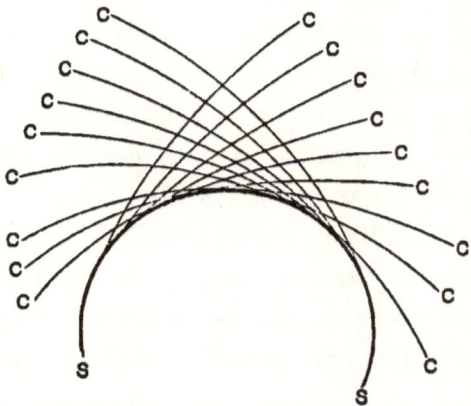

Every line, whether straight or curved, may be described as produced by the motion of a point P — this is actually the case when it is drawn by a pencil — and consequently the equation which describes the direction of a curve at any place may also be read as describing the direction of the motion of P at that place. Equations usually speak a perfectly unambiguous language, but in singular solutions an exception arises; the equation which describes the direction of motion at that point of any C where it touches S will be equally satisfied by P either continuing to move along its C, or at that point leaving the C and moving along S. So that the equation which describes the direction of the motion of P at any point of S does not absolutely determine its path, but leaves undetermined which of two paths it is to take, those paths being along curves of unlike kinds.

Where there is thus mechanical indetermination, there is, or may be, room for voluntary determination to enter. An agency like the Will, which is not properly a force, inasmuch as it cannot exert energy, may nevertheless determine the motion of a point along one of these two curves rather than the other. It is no objection to this that the indetermination shown in a singular solution cannot be realised under experimental conditions. It is impossible to do this, just as it is impossible to make a cone stand on its apex. But it does not seem by any means impossible that it may be realised among molecular or atomic actions.

argument appears of much importance, as showing that absolute determinism is not a mathematical truth. But it is not likely that it suggests the actual *modus operandi* of Freedom. The processes of life are not mechanical, and its laws are not resultants from the physical and chemical properties of the substances of which the organism is composed. Even if all physiological processes could be referred to chemical laws, this would not be true of the morphological processes which build up tissues and organs; and though it might conceivably be true that the law of Habit, in virtue of which every action tends to become easier with repetition, and to repeat itself, was a merely physical law like that whereby "streams their channels deeper wear";[1] yet the law of heredity, whereby habits and tendencies of all kinds, both active and formative, tend to be reproduced in the offspring, cannot be merely physical and mechanical. In all life, even the merely organic life of vegetables, there is something as absolutely inscrutable as the ultimate properties of matter; and it seems probable, though not capable of demonstration, that a certain limited indeterminism comes into play in the living tissues of organisms. As Sabatier reminds us, we do not there find, either in form or in function, the rigid uniformity of inorganic nature. Variation, though generally very slight, is universal; no two trees in a forest, no two leaves on a tree, are

---

[1] "Time but the impression stronger makes,
    As streams their channels deeper wear."—BURNS.

exactly alike; the same is probably true of the physiological processes of all organisms; and even if Darwin's theory of the origin of all organic forms by natural selection among spontaneous variations is unsatisfactory and insufficient, he has at least made it obvious that it is this fact of variability which makes the evolution of organic forms possible. It is asserted, no doubt, by those with whom absolute determinism is an article of scientific faith, that organic variations are absolutely determined, partly by differences and changes in the environment of the organism, and partly by the laws of its development. This may be true. It is at present, and may ever remain, impossible to prove either absolute determinism, or a certain limited indeterminism, in the organic world. Sabatier only insists that his opinion is as tenable as that of his opponents, and that the facts of organic variation give it support.

It may be mentioned that, according to Darwin, the immediate effect of a change in the environment of an organism, whether animal or vegetable, is usually not to produce any special variation, but to promote an indefinite variability. In crystallisation it is different; when the environment of crystals is changed by introducing some slight change into the chemical constitution of the liquid from which they are precipitated, the change in the form of the resulting crystals, if any, is definite.

But even if we altogether reject the idea of a certain limited indetermination in vital actions generally, this will not disprove the possibility of indetermination and freedom, also limited, in sensitive and conscious beings like the higher animals; and still more in a self-conscious being like Man. Sensation, consciousness, and self-consciousness, are such wonderful phenomena, and so totally unlike anything which can be imagined as properties of mere matter, that it would seem rather probable than otherwise if they should be accompanied by other wonderful properties, especially by this of free self-determination.

I go on to state Delbœuf's theory of the *modus operandi* of this free self-determination. He says: "Freedom disposes of time. This, as we shall see, is sufficient. We consequently define a free being as one which possesses the power of suspending its activity until the moment chosen by itself. A free being is thus a reservoir of force (or, more correctly, energy) in a state of tension, which it can transform at pleasure into actually working energy (*forces vives*). . . . This transformation of latent energy, or energy in the form of tension, is effected without any increase or decrease in the total energy of the system" of which the free being forms a part.

This appears by far the most luminous suggestion yet made on the subject, and I only wonder that, with his knowledge of natural science, Delbœuf has left it as a bare suggestion, and not worked it out into further detail. With the help of modern physiology, however, this is not difficult.

We know that the greater part of our life goes on in unconsciousness, and in total independence of the Will; the Will only enters, as it were, occasionally to control and regulate. Thus the lungs perform their function of breathing without any action of the Will, and without exciting consciousness; and in walking, our legs continue to move though we may be absorbed in the profoundest reverie, and they cease to move only in obedience to a voluntary determination like that which at first set them moving. These facts of ordinary consciousness interpret the results of anatomy and physiology. The involuntary, or what physiologists call reflex, actions of the nervo-muscular system are found to increase in force when, by some accident, or as the result of experiment, they are withdrawn from the influence of the brain, which is the organ of the Will. A case has often been quoted where an injury to a man's spinal cord made it incapable of conducting either sensible impressions to, or motor impulses from, the brain; so that the sufferer had neither sensation in, nor control over, his lower extremities; yet when the sole of his foot was tickled, he kicked more forcibly than he would have done if the nervous connections had been unimpaired. Experiments on animals yield similar results, and establish the conclusion that the relation of the voluntary and conscious forces, which have their seat in the brain, to the involuntary and unconscious forces, which have their seat chiefly in the spinal cord, is regulative, and, for the most part, inhibitory. To go back to our former illustration, it may be compared to the relation of the engineer to the steam-engine; for this also is regulative and inhibitory. The engineer controls the engine, not by impelling or ceasing to impel it by any force in his own organism, but by permitting, or refusing to permit, the steam to flow into the cylinder, and by directing it on the one side or the other of the piston.

The way in which it is probable that the Will really acts is, however, quite unlike this. There appears to be conclusive evidence that the animal system has the power of storing energy, which can be afterwards liberated for the purpose of doing muscular work.[1] The seat of this stored energy is probably the substance of the muscles; and the Will determines muscular action by determining whether, and at what time, this stored energy shall be transformed, by the contraction of the muscles, into actually working energy. It is true that the determination of the will is conveyed to the muscle, not by any immediate action, but by a current of nervous energy sent downwards from the brain; the sending of which current involves a transformation of energy, and is as truly a physical agency as the opening or closing of a steam-valve by the engineer. It seems probable

---

[1] For the facts which prove this, see Carpenter's *Human Physiology*; also the account of the experiments of Fick and Wislicenus on muscular work, in the *Philosophical Magazine*, June 1866.

that the transformation of an infinitesimally small quantity of nervous energy is effected in the brain, by the immediate act of the Will, from the stored or static form (analogous to electricity in a Leyden jar), into the kinetic or current form (analogous to electricity running along a wire); this determines the flow, from the brain down to the muscle, of a nervous current;—which current, however, is almost exclusively supplied, not from the brain, but by the transformation, from the static into the current form, of the energy that was stored in the nerve itself;—and this in its turn determines the transformation of the stored energy of the muscles themselves into working energy. Here are three successive transformations of energy, whereof the first and the second each determines that which succeeds it, and is probably almost infinitesimally smaller than that which it determines. This presents an obvious analogy to the case already mentioned, of the engineer, with a turn of his hand, starting a small steam-engine which starts a large one. The number of links in the chain of causation may be greater than this, but it appears scarcely possible that they can be very many. It is at least conceivable that in the original determination within the brain, the Will may be free, in that absolute sense in which Delbœuf, in the passage first quoted, defines Freedom, either to effect or not to effect that transformation of energy on which depends the sending downwards of the nervous current that sets the muscle in action; for we cannot doubt that energy is stored in the brain and in the entire nervous system, as well as in the muscles; and that the motion of every nerve-current, as of every electric current, involves the transformation of energy from some other form into that represented by the current.

It may, as we have remarked before, be objected that this is a similar case to that of the engineer, who starts or stops his engine by a turn of his hand, which is a mechanical action, involving an exertion of force and a transformation of energy; and consequently that it brings us no nearer to understanding how the actions of the muscular system, which are mechanical, can be directed by the Will, which is not a mechanical agency, and cannot supply energy. But to this it may be replied, that, as we have seen, the proportion which the muscular force exerted by the engineer bears to the force of his engine, may be diminished without limit, provided only that it does not become absolutely null. We know nothing whatever of the *modus operandi* of the Will in determining the transformation of stored energy in the brain into a nerve-current; but we are safe in asserting that it bears no resemblance to that of the engineer, and does not consist in anything like moving a lever; and I see nothing improbable in the belief that the Will may exercise its directive and regulative function without the exertion of any energy whatever. When man's mechanical art can diminish the magnitude of the directing force infinitesimally, provided that it is not absolutely reduced to nothing, it seems probable that it may be absolutely reduced to nothing by the vital powers of the organism, which infinitely excel all human art in subtlety. Boussinesq's illustration from geometry, though not suggesting how this can be done, appears to show that it implies no mathematical absurdity.

The freedom of which we speak is emphatically called Moral Freedom; all moralists agree that Moral Freedom is manifested in self-control, and practically means the power of self-control. We now see the physiological ground and interpretation of this. Self-control consists, primarily, in the control, by the Will, of muscular actions which, without such control, would have gone on in response to stimuli, as in the case of the patient who kicked when tickled on the soles of his feet, though unconscious of the tickling. Will—or, if this word is thought inapplicable, voluntary action—is developed in animals to this extent, namely, of voluntary control over their own muscular motions.

In my opinion, the step in development which separates the human from the highest animal intellect, consists in acquiring the power of directing thought at will.[1] On this depends the power of abstraction, and with it the ability to use arbitrary signs, and the faculty of language; for, as Max Müller has shown

[1] Max Müller, in a letter in *Nature* of the 14th July 1887, speaks of this view as being at least worthy of consideration.

in his recent work on the *Science of Thought*, every word in its origin is a result of abstraction.

These considerations throw light on the evolution of Will and self-consciousness. Mind has been evolved from sensation as from a germ. We have no means of knowing how far down in the animal scale sensation really begins; but it appears certain that in its first beginning, sensation exists only as a guide to muscular action; and that all muscular actions, such as the motion of the mouth in closing on food, are performed in immediate response to a nervous stimulus. But when the conditions of life so change that the animal can no longer obtain food by merely closing its mouth upon it, as a sea-anemone does, but has to use some of the arts of a hunter; and when at the same time the first developed single ganglion further develops into a rudimentary brain; then when the nervous stimulus, coming probably from the eye, reaches the brain, and the animal has to watch its prey instead of at once closing upon it, it is probable that the impulse to close upon its prey, inherited from the ages before its brain was developed, is still transmitted; but is counteracted by an inhibitory impulse engendered in the brain itself, and throwing the nervo-muscular system into a state of strain between the two opposing impulses; while at the same time the arrest of muscular action heightens the consciousness which the sensory impression excites in the brain; for it is a well-known law, that consciousness is heightened when muscular action is hindered, whether by a voluntary or an involuntary cause. This counteraction of the impulse to close on the prey is the germ of voluntary self-control; this heightening of consciousness is the germ of attention, and ultimately of the power to direct thought at will, and of the consciousness of self. In this pause, produced by the opposition between the sensory impulse to rush forward and the mental determination to hold back, is contained the germ of all the self-conscious and voluntary life which constitutes Mind.[1]

This may appear fanciful, and it is not advanced as an established truth. But, though the first germs of attention and voluntary determination are probably to be found in such creatures as ants and spiders, it is scarcely an exaggeration to say that the evolution which I have endeavoured to describe may be witnessed in that very common though most interesting sight, a dog pointing. His stillness is visibly not that of rest, but of strain, as between two evenly-balanced impulses, one urging him forward and the other holding him back. Darwin suggests that this remarkable habit—which, like other acquired habits, has in some degree become hereditary—is only the exaggeration of the pause of a carnivorous animal going to rush on its prey; and he adds, that probably no one would have ever thought of teaching

---

[1] The foregoing has been suggested by Mr. Sully's review of Wundt's *Physiological Psychology* in *Mind* of January 1886.

a dog to point, unless he had noticed such a tendency.

We may be reminded that while we have offered an account of the evolution of some of the mental powers, we have taken for granted the evolution of the brain, on which the mental powers depend. This is true. Structure and Function have been evolved together, and the evolution of each was necessary to that of the other.

To return to the point where we began. I do not say that these reasonings prove the reality of indeterminism and Freedom. I do not think it admits of proof;—it is as much as we can hope for, if we can show that from the scientific point of view our opinion is as defensible as the opposite one, while the moral arguments for the doctrine of Freedom remain for what they are worth—and in my opinion they are worth very much. Professor Huxley once said— I quote from memory—that the controversy about Necessity and Freedom will always be a drawn battle, and that for all practical purposes this is equivalent to the believers in Freedom gaining the victory. I can assent to this, though Huxley is a Necessarian and I believe in Freedom; all that we can hope to do is to remove some supposed presumptions in favour of the doctrine of absolute Necessity, and some difficulties in the way of believing in Freedom, which at first sight may appear formidable, and yet disappear when really understood. I fully admit that the entire world of mere matter is, probably, "bound fast in fate"; that Freedom exists in living beings only, perhaps in none but man, and dominates only a small portion even of man's life. But we have seen with Boussinesq that absolute determinism is not universally true in mathematics, and therefore need not be universally true in nature; though it is not probable that indeterminism and Freedom actually enter in the way indicated by Boussinesq's reasoning. We have seen with Sabatier that the variability which is so remarkable in the organic world, and, according to Darwin, makes possible the evolution of organic forms, appears to show a sensible though very minute degree of indetermination in the physiological and formative, as well as the motor, actions of living beings. And we have seen with Delbœuf that the manner in which Will most probably determines action, without being itself capable of exerting motive power, is by determining the moment for the transformation of stored-up energy in the organism into active energy.

I do not deny that all this is hypothetical. We have to do with questions in which certainty—demonstrative certainty, at least—is at present unattainable, and may ever remain so. But the doctrine that Mind is bound fast in the same chain of fate with inorganic matter, is as hypothetical, and as incapable of proof, as the doctrine of a certain limited freedom of the Will. I am not now replying to those who deny the freedom of the Will on metaphysical grounds; my argument is directed against those only who deny it on grounds of physical science, and I believe that on their own grounds their argument may be refuted.

The so-called scientific argument against the possibility of Freedom has been stated already; namely, that Freedom is inconsistent with the Conservation of Energy; and I have stated my reply to it. This, however, is not all that is to be said. If it is true, as the argument implies, that no mental determination can alter the direction in which physical causation acts, much more is involved in this than the denial of Freedom. Moral Freedom was denied on metaphysical grounds before any one had thought of bringing the laws of motion and force into the argument; but, if we deny it on purely physical grounds, we must deny the possibility of Mind being an agent at all. When we shrink from pain or seek pleasure, the older Necessarianism did not think of denying that the fear of pain and the hope of pleasure, which are mental affections, are the causes of the appropriate muscular actions. But if it is true that the law of the Conservation of Energy makes it impossible for any mental determination to change the action of physical causation, then mental determination can neither produce nor influence muscular motion, and consciousness misleads us in making us believe that our mental determinations— our desires and our fears—determine our bodily actions.

To mere common sense this conclusion must

appear impossible and absurd. Nevertheless, it has been accepted by Professor Huxley[1] and many others of the same school, and is known as the theory of Automatism. It may be thus stated: "Consciousness may no doubt be a result of physical action, as when an object of sight affects the nerves of the eye. But when Consciousness appears, in its turn, to be a cause of physical action, as when a determination of will to move is followed by bodily motion, this is an illusion. Such mental determination is nothing more than the accompaniment and the sign of the flow of a nervous current in the brain, which might have produced the same result of muscular motion without any consciousness being awakened. The action of the legs of the patient who kicked violently in response to tickling which he could not feel, is the type of all nervous and muscular action whatever. All muscular action, whether conscious or unconscious, goes on as if in unconsciousness."

This is, no doubt, a paradox; but many paradoxes are true. To go no farther than our present subject, it is a paradox that Will cannot produce nervous or muscular energy; yet it is all but certain that Will cannot produce energy, and can at most only direct it. But the paradox which the theory of Automatism requires us to believe, is not only great, but enormous

---

[1] See his address on Automatism at the Belfast Meeting of the British Association, as published in the *Fortnightly Review*, November 1874.

and monstrous. If Automatism is true, then consciousness is mere surplusage, and not a cause, but only a sign, of physical action; and all human history might, without violation of any law of causation, have gone on in unconsciousness; the development of art, science, and faith might have appeared to go on with unconscious puppets for actors, without a throb of pain or a glow of pleasure; wars might have been waged without ambition, pictures painted and statues carved without a sense of beauty, music composed and performed without a sense of harmony, science built up without a love of truth, and prayer uttered without hope or fear—all as the result of nervous action never translating itself into consciousness.[1] Rather than assent to such a paradox as this, I should believe with Sir John Herschel, what is scarcely a paradox at all, that the Will has the power of creating energy to an infinitesimally small amount; though, as I have shown, I do not think this is necessary to a belief in the freedom and self-determining power of the Will.

It may be said that a *reductio ad absurdum*, however forcible, is worth little outside the domain of pure

---

[1] This is not my *reductio ad absurdum* of automatism; it is the statement of automatists themselves. Lange says: "All the acts and movements of mankind, of individual persons as well as of nations, might go on exactly as they do now, though nothing resembling a thought or a sensation were to occur in any one of those individuals." Quoted from Lange's "Geschichte des Materialismus" in Kennedy's *Natural Theology and Modern Thought*, p. 74. See the conclusion of this chapter.

mathematics and abstract logic. I do not assent to this; but a conclusive direct refutation of the theory of Automatism has been given by Mr. Romanes, a writer who is, I believe, beyond any suspicion of theological or metaphysical prejudice. It is simply this:—that if Consciousness were only an effect without being a cause, and were consequently mere surplusage, it never could have been evolved at all. Whether it is true or not that "natural selection among spontaneous variations" has been the chief cause of vital evolution, it is impossible to doubt that all vital evolution has been effected under the law of natural selection; and natural selection cannot perfect a useless function, which Consciousness would be if Automatism were true.

It is to be observed that, for the purpose of this argument, we are to understand Consciousness as including all feelings whatever, from those of the lowest animal in which sensation exists at all, up to the most highly developed mental consciousness of man. The fundamental and ultimate mystery is not Thought, but Sensation—the fact that living tissue becomes sensitive.

It is not denied by any that matter acts on Consciousness: this is the case in all sensation and perception. Now, it is in accordance with all the analogies of physical science that Consciousness should be able, conversely, to act on matter; for every effect in the physical world is in general capable of acting, conversely, as a cause. Thus, mechanical motion, electricity, and heat, may each of them be a cause of either of the others, and may also be in turn their effect. Action and reaction are equal and contrary; and from this it follows that cause and effect may exchange places, and the direction of the action be reversed.

It may be said that this reasoning is irrelevant, because motion, electricity, and heat all belong to the same order of being, but Consciousness is altogether unique. I reply that the fact of Consciousness being sufficiently kindred with the physical forces to be acted on by them, appears to be a reason for expecting that it may be able to act on them in turn. But if this presumption is rejected, then I reply that the unique and unparalleled nature of Consciousness is not a reason for thinking that it can be without effect, as taught by the automatic theory, but rather for expecting it to be accompanied by other wonderful powers, like Will and Freedom.

These, however, are but presumptions: and I go on to show how the character of the Will as a Cause becomes a direct affirmation of Consciousness.

It is admitted that Consciousness tells nothing of the causal agency whereby muscular action follows on the determination of the Will to produce it. In the act of writing, for instance, I am conscious of the intention to write the words, and of the act of writing the words; but Consciousness tells nothing of the causal link between these two, consisting in the nervous current sent down from the brain to the muscles of the hand. If I know anything about this, I have learned it from anatomists and physiologists. But in purely mental action, all the links in the chain of causation are within Consciousness. When will determines thought, or when thoughts or feelings determine each other, or when either of these determines will, the relation between the cause and the effect is directly affirmed by Consciousness. All other knowledge of causation is inferential, but this is a direct and immediate intuition. Here is what appears to be absolutely conclusive evidence of the independent action of Mind; though, of course, it tells nothing directly of the action of Mind on matter.

After all, the automatic theory, even were it proved to demonstration, would clear up no difficulty. Matter acts on Consciousness when we feel, see, or hear anything: this is denied by none, although no science can ever explain how it is possible. Automatism leaves this question untouched; and the mystery is not deepened if the converse is also true; if it is true, as men instinctively believe, that Consciousness, in the form of Will, is able to act on matter through muscular motion.

It appears to be generally believed that Automatism is fundamentally identical with the older Necessarianism, and differs from it only in being strengthened by a powerful argument drawn from physical science. Professor Huxley, in his well-known address on Automatism, appeared to describe himself as only bringing new arguments for the old Necessarian doctrine which has been extensively, however erroneously, incorporated into theology. This, however, is a misconception. Metaphysical Necessarianism did not deny the existence of Will. It may be said that a Will which is not free is a contradiction in terms;—that to deny the freedom of the Will is to deny its existence;—but this is mere rhetoric. Will means the action of the Mind, as determined by motives, towards the attainment of a purpose. The older metaphysical Necessarians maintained that the Will has no truly self-determining power: that its determinations necessarily depend on whatever motive happens at the moment to be the strongest. But they did not deny the reality of voluntary action; and in affirming it they affirmed the spontaneous belief of all men, that the Will is an agent, which is able to act on the world of matter through muscular motion; in other words, that Consciousness, or Mind, though not itself physical, is capable of becoming a link in the chain of physical cause and effect; or when this was denied, as it was by Leibnitz, and from a different point of view by Malebranche,[1] it was denied by some theory which preserved the independent agency of Mind or Will.

But Automatism, which is the doctrine of Physi-

---

[1] Leibnitz was a Necessarian. I do not know whether Malebranche would have called himself so; but he also maintained the reality of the human Will, while denying its efficiency in the world of matter.

cal, as distinguished from Metaphysical, Necessity in mental action, denies to Mind any agency, or causative power, whatever;—Automatism teaches that the supposed agency of Mind is an illusion; that the agents in what is believed to be mental action are only currents in the nerves of the brain; that all such action goes on as if in unconsciousness; and that Consciousness is related to the nervous apparatus of the brain, only as music to the instrument which produces it.

Now, if this theory is shown to be possibly false, and certainly unproved and impossible to be proved, all arguments from the side of dynamical science, against the possibility of mental self-determination and Moral Freedom, disappear. The dynamical argument against Freedom is that the intervention of such an agent as a free Will in the world of matter would involve either the creation or the destruction of energy, and would thus be inconsistent with the law of its conservation; but this argument is equally good against any agency whatever of Mind or Will in the world of matter, and is consequently no special objection to the agency of a free self-determining Will. From a physical point of view the difficulty of the action of Will on matter is the same in the case of the merest beast that ever tore fruit off a tree under the impulse of hunger, as in that of man when acting with the most deliberate wisdom; and in both, it appears to be as nearly proved as the nature of the case allows, that Consciousness, or Mind, in the form of Will, is able to direct the action of force without creating or destroying energy.

If, then, the dicta of instinct and common sense are scientifically true—if Consciousness can act on matter, and desire and fear can determine bodily action—all arguments from physical science against the possibility of Moral Freedom are irrelevant and worthless; and the question whether human action is indeed "bound fast in fate" like that of mere matter, is left to be decided, or to remain undecided, on the old metaphysical, moral, and theological ground.

Further conclusions of the highest importance follow from this. If Will is a reality and not an illusion, room is left for intercourse in prayer between God and the soul of man, and spiritual religion is possible and reasonable. And if Life and Mind are not bound in absolute mechanical rigidity, there is room, even in a dispensation from which miracle is excluded, for actions of special Divine Providence in human life and history. It is not true that human free-will, Providential action, and answers to prayer are of the nature of miracle, and are therefore excluded under the present dispensation;—there is room for them under the dispensation of natural law.

For what is here written on the difference and contradiction between the old metaphysical Necessarianism and the new Automatism, I have to express my obligation to the Rev. James Houghton Kennedy's *Natural Theology and Modern Thought*, Lecture V.[1]

[1] Donnellan Lectures, delivered before the University of Dublin, 1888, 1889. Hodder and Stoughton, 1891.

CHAPTER XI.

THE REALITY OF KNOWLEDGE.

[This chapter reproduces the substance of the following papers by the present writer:—"The Reality of Knowledge," contributed to the Proceedings of the Victoria Institute; "Evolution and Man's Faculty of Knowledge," contributed to the *Homiletic Magazine*, and republished in *Christianity and Evolution* (Nisbet, 1887); and "The Admissions of Agnosticism," a review in the *British Quarterly*, July 1885, of Dr. Matheson's work *Can the Old Faith live with the New?*]

ALL questions of philosophy either begin from, or run up into, the question — What is the nature of the faculty whereby we attain to knowledge? And all questions of religious philosophy either begin from, or run up into, the question, which is included in the former—What is the nature of the faculty whereby we apprehend that which is directly made known neither in external Observation nor in internal Consciousness? Self is made known in Consciousness, and the external world in Observation; but whence comes the idea of that which underlies and transcends them both—that which, in the world of sense, is the Infinite, and in the world made known by Consciousness, is the Divine?

I believe that "the solving word" for the problem as to our knowledge of both the natural and the spiritual worlds, is suggested in a well-known stanza by Goethe, of which the following is a translation. I have inserted some words, marked in brackets, which do not represent anything in the original.

> Were not the eye with light endowed,
> How could we gaze on sun (or cloud)?
> Had we no power Divine within,
> How could the heavenly glory win
> Our spirits (and reprove our sin)?

We can understand Divine things because there is something Divine in our nature;—because, as Saint Paul said to the Athenians in the words of a poet of their own, *we are the offspring of God.*[1] And we can understand natural things because we are a part, and, as the doctrine of Evolution teaches, a product, of the world of Nature. Some one has said that the most wonderful thing about the natural world is its comprehensibility by our intellect; but this is a misconception. The material world, the world of life, and the world of mind, are all wonderful; but when conscious Intelligence has been evolved in beings which inhabit, and form part of, a universe of matter and force, which exists, moves, and changes, in space and time, it is no additional marvel that

[1] Acts xvii. 28.

such Intelligence should, in its degree, be able to understand that universe.

It is probable that this would have been always seen, but for the prevalence of false metaphysical views of the nature of Mind and its relation to the world of matter. The necessities of thought and language demand distinct names for matter and mind, and for properties, functions, and actions belonging to the physical and to the mental orders; and before thought had learned to correct its own errors, the belief arose that where there are distinct names there must be distinct things to bear the distinct names. This belief in distinct substances of Body and Mind (using the word substance in its primary metaphysical sense) has, until our own time, been generally regarded as a necessary part of both religious and philosophical orthodoxy; but philosophy is now inclined to reject it as false, and theology is beginning to see that it has no theological value. I hope to show, however, that it is far short of the truth to call this doctrine unimportant; I hope to show that its disproof will remove great difficulties from the way of rational philosophy and rational theology.

The doctrine of the absolute distinction between mind and matter, or what I call the metaphysical conception of the nature of Mind, was, of course, always confronted with the difficulty of understanding how the mind and the body, being supposed to belong to totally distinct and unlike orders of being, could act on each other at all. This, however, was accepted as a fact, impossible to deny, but altogether mysterious; and it is true that the mysteriousness of a fact is no reason for denying it. There is mystery at the ground of all being whatever.

All physiological research, however, tends to prove that as sensation has no existence apart from the nerves, so consciousness and thought have no existence apart from the brain. No doubt, as Dr. Tyndall has said, the connection of thought with molecular action in the brain is "unthinkable," or, in common language, unintelligible; not only unknown, but impossible to be known by such faculties as ours. But the ultimate mystery is not the perfected evolution of Mind; the ultimate mystery is the origin of sensation—the fact of organic tissue becoming sentient; and the mysteriousness of this is not lessened by the fact that there is no sharp separation between sentient and insentient life, similar to that existing between life and the inorganic forces. Given, however, the fact that living tissue becomes sentient, the development of a brain out of primitive ganglia and nerve fibres, and of thought out of sensation, are mysterious only as all vital development is mysterious; but, to quote Tyndall's passage on the relation of Mind to brain, with the change of the words marked in italics—" The passage from the physics of the *nerves* to the corresponding facts of *sensation* is unthinkable. Granted that a definite *sensation* and a definite molecular action in the *nerves* occur simultaneously, we do not possess the intellectual organ, nor, apparently, the rudiments of such an organ, which would enable us to pass, by a process of reasoning, from the one to the other. They appear together, but we do not know why."

But though all this is totally inscrutable, there are other questions respecting Mind, on which I believe it will be found that the doctrine of Evolution throws much light.

At an early period, the doctrine that knowledge comes through sensible perception was formulised in the well-known saying: "There is nothing in the intellect but what was previously in the sense." But this, even if true, was evidently an incomplete statement; and Leibnitz modified it thus: "There is nothing in the intellect but what was previously in the sense, except the intellect itself." This addition to the old axiom is so self-evident that it may appear scarcely worth making; but it raises the entire question of the relation between the two factors of our knowledge, namely, the impressions which come through the organs of sense, and the intellect on which the impressions are made. This is a vast problem, and it is perhaps not too much to say that all philosophical work since the time of Leibnitz has been occupied in approximating to its solution.

The philosophy of Kant, which its author rightly named the Critical Philosophy, begins with the investigation of this problem; and its result is briefly as follows :—The material of knowledge is contributed by the senses, and the form by the Mind itself. There are forms of thought (or rather of intuition), especially Time, Space, and Causation (or the relation of cause and effect), which belong to the structure of the Mind, and constitute moulds, as it were, wherein the material furnished by sensation is cast into form ; —or, to use a more instructive illustration, the forms of thought are related to the impressions of sense, somewhat as the formative agency which builds up the organism is related to the materials which are supplied in its food.

The distinctness of these forms of thought, at least those of Space and Time, from mere impressions of sense, is shown by the fact that we perceive them to be universal and necessary. All objects are presented in Space, and all events occur in Time; but if we imagine all objects to be absent, Space will still remain; and if we imagine all events to be absent, Time will still remain.

Kant appears to have concluded that these are forms of thought and nothing more; that their existence and meaning as forms of thought can no more be accounted for than the properties of matter; and that although our mental constitution compels us to perceive, and to think of, things and events according to the forms of Space, Time, and Causation, yet these have no reality external to the Mind which so perceives and thinks. It is difficult to see how any other conclusion is logically possible, consistently with the metaphysical conception of Mind which was received in Kant's time, according to which, although the mind comes into contact with the external world in sensation, yet in thought it is shut in and isolated. And from this the passage is easy and obvious, to the conclusion that absolute Truth—truth which is true independently of any faculties of ours—is unattainable by us, and may possibly have no existence. Thus with Kant the conclusions of the speculative reason led to speculative scepticism. Although he endeavoured to escape from the absolute scepticism of the pure, or speculative, reason by means of what he called the practical reason,—that is to say, the sense of Duty as distinguished from the sense of Truth,—this part of his philosophy is not generally thought to be successful; and it appears extremely improbable that if absolute, super-sensual, and Divine Truth is opened to man through the sense of Duty, it should be made known in no other way. It is certainly much more likely that when once our eyes are opened to the light of Heaven, everything will be seen to shine with it.

Kant's conclusion that absolute Truth is unattainable, is what is now called Agnosticism; and, so far as I am aware, the agnostics of our time have made no advance on this part of his philosophy.

Let us now approach the subject from a different point of view; not that of abstract metaphysics, but nearer to that of natural history; and let us try to discover how thought, and thoughts, have been actually evolved.

As Pascal said, long before the word Agnostic was invented, absolute consistent doubt is impossible; the constitution of our faculties makes it so. Whatever our theoretical conclusions may be, we cannot be consistent doubters in practice; we cannot act as if we believed the recollection of the past to be a dream, and the expectation of the future an illusion. But further; mere blank Agnosticism is not only practically impossible, but logically absurd; it is contradicted, as we shall see farther on, in the very attempt to state it.

To be an absolute agnostic, it would be necessary to have sensations only, without any consciousness of them; or, if this is regarded as a contradiction in terms, though I think it is not so, let us say, only sensations which are nothing more than sensations; sensations without, on the one hand, the power of remembering them, or on the other, the power of perceiving the objects which excite them. All who in any degree admit the truth of Evolution will admit that Sensation is the root and germ out of which Mind is evolved; and probably there are beings having sensations which are nothing more than sensations; but they exist only among the lower ranks of the animal creation, such as oysters and limpets, which have a nervous system, and probably some dim sensations, but almost certainly no true mental life. They have no power to transcend their own sensations; for them, the universe is limited to self. But when a rudimentary mental nature comes into being, and mere sensation develops into the power of perception;—when from a sensation the animal learns to infer the existence of an external object which excites the sensation, whether food, or another animal by which it may itself be eaten; and when past sensations are remembered as real though no longer present; it has been brought to knowledge which contains an element transcending sensation, and not implied in it.

With respect to Memory, it is not, I believe, denied by any, that belief in the reality of the past, and in the general trustworthiness of Memory in witnessing of the past, is an ultimate fact of mental nature. This is expressly admitted by John Stuart Mill in his *Examination of the Philosophy of Sir William Hamilton*. His words are, "Our belief in the veracity of Memory is evidently ultimate." It is curious that his admission of this truth, which is evidently not only ultimate but fundamental, should be made in a footnote; and it is remarkable that Mill, in the chapter where this note occurs, and Bishop Butler, in the essay on Personal Identity which is usually printed with his *Analogy*, should have arrived at exactly the same conclusion, though expressed in different words;—namely, that personal identity, persisting through time and change, is an ultimate fact, consisting in nothing but itself. And yet Mill began from sensation;—he endeavoured to show that the fabric of knowledge and thought is constructed out of the materials of sensation by the agency of the association of ideas; and the aim of his philosophy was to minimise the element of faith in thought. Butler, on the contrary, though by no means a transcendentalist, never lost sight of the element of faith in our thought and knowledge; and, so far as his purpose was properly philosophical, it was to insist on the importance of this element.

It is true that Memory, in its most rudimentary form, is nothing more than a continued sensation, such as the sensation of light continuing after a flash of light has passed. But in its developed form, Memory implies the belief in a past which was once present but is so no longer, and in a self which is permanent through past and present sensations. Agnosticism, pure, simple, and consistent, would require this to be denied; would deny, or leave in doubt, whether the permanent element in the self is anything but an illusion; whether the past is anything but a dream, and whether the future may be reasonably expected to arrive. But it is not possible to doubt the truth of any of these; and in the case of the reality of the self—of its personal identity and unity as opposed to its manifold states of feeling—the certainty is not only instinctive but logical; that is to say, we believe it not only as we believe in the reality of Time and Space, because belief in their reality is part of our constitution; but also because the question of the reality of the self cannot be asked until the self exists to ask it; so that its denial would not only contradict an affirmation of Consciousness, but would also contradict that logical principle which lies at the base of all reasoning, and indeed of all assertion, that a contradiction cannot be true—that a thing cannot at once be existent and non-existent, and a proposition cannot be at once true and false. This is not offered as a new demonstration; it is only a restatement of that fundamental axiom of all philosophy which Descartes formulated in the words "Cogito, ergo sum," "I think, therefore I exist";—that is to say, the existence of self is made known and proved, not in mere Sensation but in Thought. It seems to me that this saying is improved by translating it into English, and thus bringing into prominence the personal pronoun.[1]

Physical and metaphysical knowledge are both equally real; and as metaphysical knowledge, or knowledge of what is made known in Consciousness, begins with the consciousness of self, so physical knowledge, or knowledge of external nature, begins with the discovery of the existence of a world

---

[1] It has been said that this is not a proof but a *petitio principii*, because it involves the assumption that whatever thinks must exist. But this mistakes the true significance of Descartes' saying. It is not meant as logical demonstration, but goes deeper than demonstration. In demonstration, from truths already known we infer other truths; but this saying is merely a statement of the way in which, as a matter of fact, the self becomes aware of itself as a self.

external to self. The belief in the existence of the external world is secondary (in logical order, though probably not in the order of development) to the belief in the permanent self; for consciousness of self is, and the belief in an external world is not, a condition of all thought whatever. But they have not only the same degree but the same kind of certainty. We do not here need to enter on the question of the nature of material substance. As Berkeley showed long ago, the deepest metaphysical analysis proves that matter can be interpreted only in terms of sensation and thought; and it is equally true that the highest physical science of our time tends to merge the idea of matter in that of force. There is an unsolved and insoluble mystery about the nature of the material world, no less than about the nature of our personality. As self is made known to itself by the diversity of its sensations, so is the external world made known by the experience of a multitude of sensations (it would be more intelligible, though less accurate, to say perceptions), whereof the coexistences and successions are not determined by our own thought or our own will. The belief in the existence of an external world, is the affirmation of the judgment that what does not originate within must come from without; and this, like the belief in personal identity, is not only instinctive but logical; it cannot be denied without self-contradiction.

This belief is independent of any opinion as to the nature of the external world. If, with Mill, we refuse to form any opinion on the subject, and confine ourselves to stating the mere fact that we know the external world as consisting only of "permanent possibilities of sensation," still it makes itself known to us as external;—external, that is, to our consciousness and our will.

I may remark here, though it is a digression from the main argument, that although the progress of physical science, which has extended our knowledge of the material world so marvellously beyond mere sensible perception, tends to merge the idea of matter in that of force, yet it gives no support to that denial of the existence of material substance, which Mill, and, I believe, other agnostics, have adopted from Berkeley. Science reveals an entire world of realities which are not objects of sensible perception; such as the waves of light, the vibrations of heat, the molecular tensions which constitute magnetism and electricity, and the atomic structure of matter: these are as real as waves in water or stratification in rocks, yet, not being actual or possible objects of perception, their reality seems to be denied by the Berkeleyan theory, which teaches that things exist only as they are perceived.[1] And there is also this kindred difficulty;—If it is true that material things exist only as they are perceived, what was there to constitute the being of the world of matter when nothing had as yet been created except the primæval nebula, and no sentient or thinking being had been called into existence to

---

[1] As Berkeley tersely puts it, their *esse* is *percipi*.

perceive the world around it? Berkeley, I believe, would have replied that the existence of all these consists in being perceived and known by God. But though I am a convinced Theist, this appears to me totally unsatisfactory, unless we are to maintain that God perceives objects in the same way that we do; which would be absurd; for the Divine knowledge of things is immediate, while ours is the result of a process in the complex apparatus of the organs of sense, and of the nerves and the ganglionic substance of the brain. I am confirmed in the belief that this argument against Berkeleyanism is of some weight, by the fact that Mill, whose metaphysical acuteness will not be questioned, appears to have endeavoured to reply to it by anticipation. I refer to his attempt to get rid of the theory of a luminiferous ether in which the waves of light are formed;—he called it a mere metaphysical figment. Mill was influenced in this great error by a thinker far inferior to himself in depth, namely Auguste Comte, whose hatred of everything that he labelled as metaphysical amounted to fanaticism.

We share the knowledge of the self and of the external world with the higher animals; but with the specially human power of directing thought at will, a third element enters into knowledge; namely, a sense of something which underlies and transcends both the self and the external world; something which is infinite as opposed to their finitude, changeless as opposed to their changefulness, and necessary, or absolute, as opposed to their contingency. The earliest and crudest form of this intuition is the sense of merely natural, or spatial, infinity; and this is not a generalisation or an inference; it is, like the intuition of the self and of the external world, attained by the spontaneous activity of the mind. On this subject I will quote some remarkable words from Max Müller, though he appears to attribute to the mind's passive capacity what I should rather attribute to its unconscious activity.

"We have accepted the primitive savage with nothing but his five senses. These five senses supply him with a knowledge of finite things; our problem is how such a being ever comes to speak or think of anything not finite but infinite. I answer without any fear of contradiction, that it is his senses which give him his first impression of infinite things, and force him to the admission of the Infinite. Everything to which his senses cannot perceive a limit is, to the primitive savage, or to any man in an early stage of intellectual activity, unlimited or infinite. Man sees—he sees to a certain point, and there his eyesight breaks down. But exactly where his sight breaks down, there presses upon him, whether he likes it or not, the perception of the unlimited or Infinite. It may be said that this is not perception in the ordinary sense of the word. No more it is; but still less is it mere reasoning. In perceiving the Infinite, we neither count, nor measure, nor compare, nor name; we know not what it is, but we know that it is, and we know it because we actually feel it, and are brought in contact with it."

"The more we advance, the wider, no doubt, grows our horizon; but there never is, and never can be, to our senses, a horizon, unless as standing between the visible and finite on the one side, and the Invisible and Infinite on the other. The Infinite, therefore, instead of being merely a late abstraction, is really implied in the earliest manifestation of our sensuous knowledge."[1]

At a later period, the sense of the Infinite is forced on man, not only by perception as at first, but also by thought. It was said by Mill, that "the laws of nature cannot account for their own origin"; nor, we may add, for their own existence. Experience suggests questions which it cannot answer, nor find any data for answering. So soon as man learns to ask, Whence is the order of things, and what is the ground of its existence? What is the Power that manifests itself in the sun, in the wind, and in the lightning? he has already recognised the existence of that which underlies and transcends the visible universe, and, by definition, belongs to a supersensible world. The thought of the Invisible is suggested by the perception of the visible; and, as the visible is finite, the Invisible is conceived of as the Infinite.

[1] Hibbert Lectures on the "Origin and Growth of Religion," by Professor Max Müller, pp. 38, 39.

"The process by which we reached this conclusion was itself a purely natural process. We did not reach it by any transcendentalism, we did not come to it by any mysticism; we were driven to it by the barred gate of our own experience. It was the limits of our own senses that compelled us to seek a solution of the universe which invoked the presence of a Power beyond them. Experience, and nothing but experience, was the source of our information that Nature was inadequate to account for her own existence. No transcendental logic, no mystical power of abstraction, no special faculty conversant with the things beyond experience, would ever in this matter have possessed one tithe of the authority which was wielded by the testimony of experience itself, when it told us that the domain of visible nature was too narrow and limited to account for what we see."[1]

The Invisible which we are thus compelled to recognise is identical with the Unknowable of that modern philosophy which is formulised in the writings of Herbert Spencer;—a self-existent and eternal Power, the ground of the existence of all being, mental or material, and in its essential nature absolutely inscrutable to us. Those who stop here, and assert that no further knowledge is possible to such faculties as ours, call themselves not believers but agnostics. But, as Dr. Matheson remarks, "to know that we know nothing,

---

[1] Matheson's *Can the Old Faith live with the New?* p. 59.

is already to have reached a fact of knowledge."[1] Such Agnosticism as this is not blank ignorance, but the first step out of ignorance; not blank atheism, but the first step out of atheism. Such a conclusion respecting the Invisible, the Infinite, or the Unknowable, may more properly be called naturalistic Pantheism; it nearly amounts to a recognition of what, in the theology of the eighteenth century, were called the physical attributes of Deity.

But when we seek to build on the foundation here laid, and to add to these the doctrines of Divine Will, Knowledge, and Holiness, with the possibilities of Revelation and Incarnation, agnostics meet us with the assertion that these are beyond the limits of our possible knowledge;—that, even if true, we could not know them to be true. Why not? If we can recognise the Divine Power, as the Agnosticism of Herbert Spencer teaches that we must, though he does not call it Divine, why should it be impossible for us to recognise the Divine Wisdom and Holiness? Even if it is certain—which I by no means admit—that these are made known neither in Nature nor in Consciousness, why should it be impossible for God to make them known by Revelation? On his own principles, one who asserts nothing about the Invisible Power of the Universe except that it is inscrutable, ought not to dogmatise on the subject. Whether dogmatic belief is reasonable, must depend on reason and evidence; but dogmatic unbelief

[1] *Can the Old Faith live with the New?* p. 356.

cannot be reasonable, because, by the terms of the case, it is not based on evidence, but on the absence of evidence.

When we consider the powers of man's mind with the view of forming an idea of the possibilities of religious knowledge, we must observe that all knowledge of mere Nature is, for this purpose, of altogether secondary—not to say infinitely small—importance, in comparison with our knowledge of Mind. The instinct which teaches us the existence of a sentient and mental nature, like our own, in our fellow-men, is obviously of a higher kind than the instincts which teach the existence of self and of the external world. Yet it is properly an instinct: it is indeed of a more purely instinctive nature than those others, because it contains no logical element. If any man were to believe that he was the only sentient being in the universe, and that all the men around him were but moving masks, this would no doubt be conclusive proof of insanity; yet, unlike the belief in the existence of self and of the external world, such a belief would contradict no logical principle, and its falsity could not be demonstrated. This instinct appears to show itself in children from the earliest dawn of intelligence, and it begins in the animal creation; for we cannot doubt that gregarious animals understand the feelings of other animals of their own species by instinctive sympathy, just as we ourselves do. This belief, no doubt, is produced by the sight of its objects, that is to say, of other beings similar to ourselves; and, when once formed, all experience confirms and justifies it. But how did the capacity for such a belief originate? The capacity for conceiving, and believing in as existent, a being with sensations and thoughts like one's own, yet not oneself, is not implied in the discovery either of the existence of self or of the external world; it appears to be a distinct endowment, unique in kind; and I maintain that the existence of this endowment contains the refutation of the entire system of dogmatic Agnosticism.

If Agnosticism means only that we have in fact attained to no knowledge transcending our experience of the things made known by sensible perception, this is not a theory or system of doctrine at all, but only a provisional conclusion or a provisional suspension of judgment. But Agnosticism, as a reasoned system, goes beyond this, and asserts not only that we have attained to no such knowledge, but that the constitution of our faculties is such as to make any such knowledge necessarily and for ever impossible of attainment by us.

The data of all our knowledge, according to this theory, consist exclusively of sensible perceptions, and the conclusions cannot belong to a world altogether transcending their data. Now it is true that in reasoning on merely physical subjects, the conclusions always remain, as it were, on the same plane of thought with their data. A planet may be discovered before it has been seen, but none the less it belongs to the same physical world with other planets; the waves of sound and light, though they cannot be directly perceived by our organs of sense, yet are shown by the reasoning which discovers them to be analogous in constitution, though with differences, to the waves of water which we see; and although such a natural law as that of the force of gravitation varying with the inverse square of the distance could not conceivably be an object of sensible perception at all, yet the law, when discovered, is not anything added to the phenomena: it is only the statement of the law under which the phenomena occur.

But it is different in reasoning about Mind. It may appear profoundly logical to assume that the conclusions of reasoning must always belong to the same order, and lie in the same plane of thought, with their data; but the fact is not so. We reason truly from human actions and words, and from human countenances and voices, which belong to the order of sensible perception, to human thought, purpose, and character, which belong to the mental and spiritual order. Now, on this power is based the possibility of our acquiring knowledge of spiritual things, and receiving a revelation. If we have an instinctive power which enables us to reason truly from data of merely sensible perception to conclusions in the world of mind and thought, it cannot be essentially impossible for us to learn, from facts made known in nature and consciousness, and from additional facts revealed in prophecy and miracle, truths infinitely transcending their data, and belonging to the spiritual and Divine world. So that no proof is shown for the assertion that religious knowledge is necessarily unattainable; the way is open to consider the evidence that may be adduced for it; and Agnosticism is but a temporary blindness, caused by too exclusive attention to merely physical data, and to mathematical methods of reasoning from them, which can never lead to conclusions transcending these data. As the mere perceptive faculty cannot attain to the truths of science, so the mere reasoning faculty cannot attain to spiritual knowledge.[1] The root of the spiritual faculty is not in the logical intellect which reasons from data in the world of nature to conclusions in the same; it is in the instinctive capacity, transcending all mere logic, whereby we learn to understand the minds, the thoughts, and the feelings of our fellow-men.

But the agnostic objection will still be made:—
"We have no reason to believe that our ideas have any resemblance to the reality of things. For anything we know, the appearances of things may be to their realities only as speech to thought, or writing to speech—a system of symbols which give information about the realities which they represent, without resembling those realities or partaking of their nature. Infinite is a word of magnitude; and if Space and Time, in which alone magnitude can be expressed, are mere forms of our own thought, we can have no

---
[1] 1 Cor. ii. 14.

reason to believe in any really existing Infinite external to ourselves. And if this is true of the world of nature, how much more certainly true is it of spiritual and Divine things!"

I reply, that granting to the utmost the unreality, or merely phenomenal character, of our knowledge of the natural world, this in no degree diminishes the certainty, and the absolute (as opposed to the merely relative) character of our knowledge of our fellow-men as resembling ourselves; and our knowledge of God, as I have endeavoured to show, is allied, not to our knowledge of Nature, but to our knowledge of Man.

But I do not admit the doctrine of the unreality of our knowledge of the external universe. In order to consider this subject, we must go back to what has been said of Kant's views on Space and Time.

I have endeavoured to show that belief in the reality of self and of the external world is not only instinctive but logical; that their truth is involved in that of those logical principles which are implied in all assertion. The same, however, is not true of the reality of Space and Time. These are forms of thought;—and there is no logical absurdity—no self-contradiction—in maintaining, with Kant, that they are nothing more than forms of thought; in other words, that by the constitution of our faculties we necessarily perceive sensations as succeeding each other in Time, and external objects as having position in Space, while we have no reason to believe that

Space and Time have any actual existence apart from our faculties of perception. So long as the doctrine of Evolution was unknown, and so long as mind and body were supposed to be altogether different though mysteriously united, the question of the objective reality of Space and Time appeared totally insoluble. But we have now learned that Mind is only a name for the sum-total of the sensory and conscious functions of the organism;—that the living conscious organism is a part, and in some sense a product, of the universe of matter and force wherein it lives;—and that the mind of man is one of many minds which have originated in the animal creation, though incomparably the most highly developed of them all. These considerations suggest with a force which to my mind is almost, if not quite, equal to demonstration, that Space and Time are forms of thought because they were originally facts of the universe. When detached portions of the universe are vitalised into animals and acquire consciousness, Space and Time, being facts of the universe, become functions of their consciousness. We have every reason to believe that animals conceive of Time and Space exactly as we do before the power of abstract thought is awakened; that every animal which is capable of desire and fear knows the difference between the future and the past; that every beast which can run on the ground or climb a tree, and every bird which can fly forward, steer its flight to right or left, and rise or sink in the air, is practically, though not consciously and theoretically, aware that there are three dimensions in Space, and no more.

The same kind of analysis applies to the relation of Causation and Force. As Time is the abstract, or absolute, which underlies all relations of succession, and Space is the abstract which underlies all relations of position, so Force is the abstract which underlies all relations of Causation; and as we acquire our idea of Space by perceiving the relation of position between objects, and that of Time by experience of the relation of succession among our feelings, so we acquire that of Force by experience of the action on us of the external world in such agencies as wind and rain, and by consciousness of our own action in turn on the external world, as when we throw a stone or light a fire.

In order to anticipate a possible difficulty, I may remark that this conclusion leaves untouched the question of the possibility of the existence of more than three dimensions in Space. It is certain that the universe of which we are part, exists and moves in only three dimensions; but I understand that researches in imaginary geometry have shown the supposition of four dimensions, or of any number up to infinity, to be tenable without logical contradiction.

It is a mere statement of fact to say that Space, Time, and Causation, are forms of thought: the question is how they have become so. Kant's conclusion, that they are ultimate facts of Mind and nothing more, was natural enough when the idea of Evolution as applied to Mind was unknown, and every fact of life and mind was directly referred to Creative Will.

Locke, writing long before the time of Kant, though he did not question the doctrine of the separate existence of Mind, yet maintained that these forms of thought are the results of experience through the perceptions. This never was quite a satisfactory explanation; even if the process of acquiring these conceptions by experience were proved to be possible, it is difficult to believe that every one can have acquired them so easily and unconsciously that the process has left no trace in the memory.

But now that the doctrine of Evolution is applied to all life, sentient as well as insentient, mental as well as organic, Locke's theory of these conceptions being derived from experience has been revived, chiefly by Herbert Spencer, but in a greatly improved form. Spencer's theory is that they are results of experience which have become forms of thought;— results of the inherited experience of the race, which have become forms of thought for the individual. This theory professes to combine all that is true in the theories of both Locke and Kant. It professes to be an explanation where Kant only offered a generalised statement, and to be a sufficient explanation where Locke offered a totally inadequate one. It is obviously a great improvement on both of the theories which it professes to combine and complete. Time, Space, and Causation, or Force, are elements of all the experience of all conscious organisms; and though experience is not consciously inherited, yet its results are inherited and pass into character; so that when organisms in the course of their evolution become in any degree intelligent, these conceptions enter into their intelligence and become part of it. It is surely a simple and natural view, that these are forms of thought which have become so by unvarying experience of them, continued through countless generations; rather than unreal modes in which Consciousness, from its dawn among the first animals that acquired the sense of sight, to its highest development in the brain of man, has been so falsified as to be compelled to understand things as they are not, and to read realities unreally. The last word of science—Evolution—thus tends to support the belief that Consciousness, being evolved among the facts of the universe, reflects them truly; and to confirm that Natural Realism which is the spontaneous belief not only of men, but, I doubt not, of beasts below us and angels above.

In adhering to Kant's Agnosticism, and denying the external objective reality of these conceptions, Herbert Spencer, and those who think with him, appear inconsistent with their own principles. Being unable to get beyond the truth that Time, Space, and Causation are, in fact, forms of thought, and regarding the mind as something distinct from the world of matter and altogether unlike it, Kant was consistent with himself in denying that these are realities of the external world. But Herbert Spencer believes that the Mind is a part, and an evolved product, of the world which surrounds it; and that these forms of thought are the result of the action of the surrounding world upon the Mind in experience. Now surely "neither the individual nor the race could have the experience wherein these ideas have originated, if the realities represented by these ideas had not existed before our experience of them began. Time, Space, and Causation are not the result, but the cause, of our experience of them. Our minds have not created, but have discovered them.

"If this is true, we have escaped from the cloud-land of metaphysics by coming out at the farther side into inductive science and common sense; and we stand again, as we stood in our unmetaphysical childhood, on the firm familiar earth and in the 'light of common day,' trusting with not only an instinctive but a rational trust, that our knowledge, having grown out of experience, truly interprets experience; that our forms of thought, being produced by the constant action of the external world on our bodily and mental organisation through countless generations, really represent the realities of the external world."

I doubt, however, whether Herbert Spencer's theory on the subject is quite satisfactory;—it seems to me that the power of receiving and assimilating experience, cannot itself be the result of experience. In other words, I believe that Intelligence, like sensation, is a primary endowment, not resolvable into anything but itself.¹ In proof of this, I will here remark that our idea of Time is one which it appears impossible for experience alone to have produced. "We naturally believe that Time is without end and without beginning: we can no more conceive an absolute beginning of Time than an absolute end. Now the pure and simple experience theory accounts, no doubt, for the belief that Time is without end, by the fact that we have never had experience of any portion of Time without another portion of Time coming after it. But this will not apply to our belief that Time is without beginning: for at the time that any one's consciousness was first awakened, he had at that moment experience of a portion of Time without having experience of any other portion of time coming before it; so that for anything that mere experience can witness to, there is nothing inconceivable in a beginning of Time. This shows that although we have obtained our knowledge of Time by direct cognition, and it has become a form of our thought by the accumulation of inherited experience, yet there is something in the conception which cannot be thus accounted for, and which can be referred only to that intelligence which is not a result of experience."²

[1] For a fuller discussion of this subject, see *Habit and Intelligence*, by the present writer, second edition (Macmillan, 1879).

[2] This passage, and the former ones in quotation marks, are

But I agree with Herbert Spencer in believing that thought derives its laws from that universe of things whereof the Mind is a part; and from this I further infer that our spontaneous conceptions agree with the reality of things, and that our knowledge has a rational basis. This escape from Agnosticism seems perfectly satisfactory; so that the philosophy of Evolution, though it is despised as being materialistic, affords a basis for belief; while those idealistic systems whereof Kant's is the type, which are constructed out of the mind itself, lead by a direct and logical path to absolute theoretical scepticism.

And if the intuitions of our Intelligence in relation to the external and visible world are true, we may consistently trust the intuitions of our moral and spiritual Intelligence, which testify to the imperative character of the moral sense.

But what is the nature and source of this moral and spiritual Intelligence? How have the best and wisest men obtained their conviction of the immutable and absolute character of the opposition between moral good and evil? I know that attempts have been made to account for this on principles derived from the world of mere Nature. I do not think any of these are successful, and I have stated my reasons for this conclusion in my former work.[1] This,

taken, with the change of a few words, from my *Habit and Intelligence*, second edition, pp. 459, 460.

[1] See *The Scientific Bases of Faith*, ch. 3.

however, I will ask:—What is the origin, and what is the significance, of that instinctive faith which expects to find Goodness at the foundation of the universe? The world wherein we live is not so sinless and so happy as to enable us to base such a faith on evidence of any common kind. Yet it shows itself not in declared believers only, but also in such agnostics as Herbert Spencer, when they call the existence of evil an anomaly and a perplexity; for it would not be so if the constitution of the universe were altogether unmoral. Such faith has no doubt been very greatly strengthened by express revelation, but it is not due to revelation in the special sense; on the contrary, we could not receive a revelation if we did not believe, independently of revelation, that *God cannot lie;*[1] and it is not from experience that we have learned this faith. And whence comes the expectation that goodness and mercy may reasonably be expected from God; the faith wherein

> We trust that God is love indeed,
> And love Creation's final law,
> Though Nature, red in tooth and claw
> With ravine, shrieks against our creed?[2]

If it is true—and I think it certain—that Space,

---

[1] Ὁ ἀψευδὴς Θεός. Titus i. 2.

[2] "Who trusted God was love indeed
     And love Creation's final law—
      Tho' Nature, red in tooth and claw
     With ravine, shriek'd against his creed."
           In Memoriam.

Time, and Force are forms of our thought because they first were facts of the physical universe to which we belong by the physical side of our being, it is equally true that this insight of Faith into the things of the spiritual world is ours because by another side of our being we belong to that spiritual world.

To return to the question with which the present chapter began : What is the nature and source of the faculty whereby it is possible for Man to attain to knowledge of the Divine ?

The Agnostic reply is that no such faculty exists ; that we must resign ourselves to total and hopeless ignorance of all that transcends the data furnished to our thought in Observation and Consciousness. The whole of the present chapter is an argument against Agnosticism, and an attempt to show that it is possible for the conclusions of thought to transcend their data.

The Gnostics of the early ages of Christianity maintained that God is made known only to particular men, or to men at particular times, and only in virtue of a specially imparted power of vision. This doctrine has never become altogether extinct, and it appears to be implied in the view of conversion set forth, with extraordinary ability and eloquence, in Drummond's *Natural Law in the Spiritual World*. I have stated, in the first four-chapters of the present work, my arguments in opposition to his view.

I am opposed alike to Gnosticism and to Agnosticism. Against Agnosticism, I maintain that we can ascend to a knowledge of the Divine; and against Gnosticism, I maintain that there is no special power, and no need for any, whereby to read the indications of the Divine in Nature and Revelation; but that such knowledge is to be attained by the right use of the powers naturally conferred on Man by the Creator, assisted by revelation, and by the guidance of the Holy Spirit of God.

It may be said that the view of the nature of Mind set forth in the present chapter is materialistic, and inconsistent with any belief in immortality. In reply to this, I agree with Herbert Spencer that Materialism and Spiritualism are not two mutually opposed systems of doctrine, but two opposite sides of the same reality. Like Oersted, the discoverer of electro-magnetism, "I am at once a materialist and a spiritualist." And as to the idea that such a view of the nature of Mind is inconsistent with belief in immortality, I reply—defining Mind, as I do, to be the sum-total of the conscious functions of the organism—that the two questions do not so much as touch each other. The "natural immortality of the soul" is no doctrine of either Reason or Revelation;—Reason neither asserts nor denies immortality, but Revelation teaches that *God* confers immortality, and *doth raise the dead*.[1] "That was not first which is spiritual, but that which is natural; and afterward, that which is spiritual."[2] From our

---

[1] Acts xxvi. 8.   [2] 1 Cor. xv. 46.

scientific point of view, we may complete Saint Paul's meaning by saying, that mere matter was first; then natural organic life, attaining its highest development in the brain of man; and finally spiritual and immortal life—the *life and immortality* which has been *brought to light* by Christ.[1] As for the question, "How are the dead raised up, and with what body do they come?" Saint Paul's answer is sufficient; our ignorance is no measure of the possibilities of creation and the resources of the Creator.[2]

To sum up the conclusions of the present chapter; I am a Natural Realist on a basis of Evolutionism, and a spiritual believer on a basis of Natural Realism. The doctrine of Evolution teaches that we are a part and a product of the world of nature; from this I infer that the fundamental realities of nature—Space, Time, and Causation—are truly reflected in our intelligence as elements of our thought; and I am consequently a Natural Realist. And because I thus believe that on the physical side of our being we are open to impressions of natural truth, I infer that on the spiritual side we are, similarly, open to impressions of spiritual and Divine truth; that our Intelligence is able truly to interpret the indications of such truth made known in Nature, Conscience, and Revelation; and on this basis of Natural Realism, I am a spiritual believer.

[1] 2 Tim. i. 10. [2] 1 Cor. xv. 35 *et seq.*

NOTE TO CHAPTER XI.

KANT ON SPACE AND TIME.

LEST it should be said that I have done injustice to Kant in my representation of his teaching on the unreality of Space and Time, I proceed to quote his words on the subject from the *Critique of Pure Reason*. The quotations are taken from "The Philosophy of Kant, as contained in extracts from his own writings, selected and arranged by John Watson, LL.D., Professor of Moral Philosophy in the University of Queen's College, Kingston, Canada."[1]

First, as to Space:—

"It is, therefore, purely from our human point of view that we can speak of Space, of extended things, *etc.* Suppose the subjective conditions to be taken away, without which we cannot have any external perception, or be affected by objects, the idea of Space ceases to have any meaning. We cannot predicate

[1] Glasgow: Maclehose and Sons, 1888.

spatial dimensions of things, except in so far as they appear in our consciousness.

* * *

The proposition that all things are side by side in Space is true only under the limitation that we are speaking of our own sensible perception. But if we more exactly define the subject of the proposition by saying that all things *as external phenomena* are side by side in Space, it will be true universally and without any exception.

* * *

We therefore affirm the *empirical reality* of Space as regards all possible external experience; but we also maintain its *transcendental ideality;* or, in other words, we hold that Space is nothing at all if its limitation to possible experience is ignored, and it is treated as a necessary condition of *things in themselves.*"[1]

Kant's conclusion as to Time is exactly similar:—

"We deny to Time all claim to absolute reality, because such a claim, in paying no heed to the form of sensible perception, assumes Time to be an absolute condition or property of things. Such properties, as supposed to belong to things in themselves, can never be presented to us in sense. From this we infer the *transcendental ideality* of Time; by which we mean that, in abstraction from the subjective conditions of sensible perception, Time is simply nothing,

---

[1] Watson, pp. 28, 29. Kant's *Kritik*, 1st ed. pp. 27, 28; 2nd ed. pp. 43, 44. I have italicised the words *external phenomena* and *things in themselves.*

and cannot be said either to subsist by itself, or to inhere in things that do so subsist." "Time is therefore nothing but the form of our inner perception."[1]

The following comment of Kant's on these his own views must be quoted:—

"The natural theologian is very careful to say that God, in His perception, is free from the limits of Space and Time. But how can this possibly be maintained, if it has previously been assumed that Space and Time are forms of things in themselves? ... If they are conditions of all existence, they must be conditions of the existence even of God. We can avoid this conclusion only by saying that Space and Time are not objective forms of all things, but subjective forms of our outer as well as of our inner perceptions"[2] (*i.e.* Space of the outer and Time of the inner perceptions).

I have stated in the foregoing chapter that I believe the Divine Mind to be independent of the conditions of Space and Time. But this, in my view, is not because such relations are unreal to God, but because His Mind transcends and includes them; unlike our minds, which are included in them. We do not and cannot know the relation of Space and Time to the Divine Mind; it may be that they have been created, like the world of matter and mind. But although God transcends the created

---

[1] Watson, pp. 34, 35. Kant's *Kritik*, 1st ed. pp. 36, 37; 2nd ed. pp. 52, 54.

[2] Watson, p. 37. Kant's *Kritik*, 2nd ed. p. 71.

universe, it is not therefore unreal to Him. The thoughts of God, as all Theists believe, infinitely transcend our thoughts, but our thoughts are not therefore unreal to God.

It appears to me that Kant's conclusions as to Space and Time are very similar to Berkeley's as to the world of matter; and that the objective reality of Space and Time is to be vindicated against Kant, and that of the material world against Berkeley, on similar grounds; namely, as being both of them affirmed by that Natural Realism, to which, as I have endeavoured to show in the foregoing chapter we are led by the doctrine of Evolution.

THE END.

Printed by R. & R. CLARK, *Edinburgh.*

www.ingramcontent.com/pod-product-compliance
Lightning Source LLC
Chambersburg PA
CBHW031958230426
43672CB00010B/2194